Show Me A
Mountain

A family adventure across Africa

Dr. Maureen Mc Mullan

author HOUSE®

AuthorHouse™
1663 Liberty Drive
Bloomington, IN 47403
www.authorhouse.com
Phone: 1-800-839-8640

Published by AuthorHouse   04/09/2013

ISBN: 978-1-4817-8647-8 (sc)

CONTENTS

DEDICATION

Maureen wrote this after our retirement to Spain in 1987 using the notes she made during the trip in 1974 and by drawing on her excellent memory. After her suicide in 1990, her manuscript spent the next twenty years in a box in the garage in Kent, but eventually I passed it over to a publisher who managed to produce a computerised draft in book form, but with quite a number of things needing correction. My good friend, the Revd. Robin Paterson who, in retirement, also spends a fair amount of his time in Spain and knows quite a lot about the background to it all, felt drawn to take on the not inconsiderable task of editing it and introducing the necessary alterations. His work has proved invaluable.

This book is dedicated to our children, Peter, Sean and Sarah Jane, who suffered greatly at her loss.

My wife Donna has helped enormously not only in proof reading and correcting but in supporting me through various stages of frustration.

Thanks are due to Adrienne Scherschel and Rebecca Carter of AuthorHouse who assisted me greatly in the final production of this book.

D Mc M.

PROLOGUE

. . . HOWLING WIND, STREAMING eyes, no sign of a track. I turned and looked back at our lonely distant Land Rover and the tiny figures of my children, hunched on their knees digging furiously round the wheels. Far in the opposite direction I saw Susan scouting on, but no reassuring wave. Head down, heavy feet, bending low against the wind, she trudged dejectedly back.

Visibility was appalling. No pole or cairn to guide us, nothing but deep soft sand, knife-edged boulders and darkness approaching. "No sense of responsibility, unnecessary danger, madness" screamed the critics in my ears.

The three children paused for breath as I approached, peering hopefully through sand-covered sunglasses, faces masked by large scarves. I shook my head; they shrugged their shoulders and carried on digging. The Sahara, like the sea, was showing us its many moods. Another thousand miles still lay ahead. The bleached white camel bones mocked me . . .

CHAPTER 1

SHOW ME A MOUNTAIN . . .

"THERE MUST BE more than work, work and the old age pension."
I beseeched Susan, a friend since university days and equally dejected
as she faced a major crossroads in her career as an obstetrician. The
rain pelted against the windows, the English summer was with us
in all its glory. Puddles collected on the lawn and the trees shook
themselves as the gale whipped up into a new frenzy. We felt caught
in an inevitable rut as we stared 40 in the face. The front door banged,
whipped out of David's hand by a sudden gust. "We have decided to
go across Africa and India, taking six months to a year." I announced,
as he stuck his head round the door. He planted a kiss on the end of
my nose. "You are on, when do we leave?"

Davidand I had talked many times about taking the children on
a long expedition, but there had always been a host of reasons why
the time was not quite right. We were both feeling restless, searching
for a new challenge. David and Jeffrey, his partner, had built their own
engineering business from scratch. We had a comfortable home and
three great children. "What next" we asked each other, "we cannot
just sit here waiting for life to slip by."

I tossed and turned in bed that night, still wide awake at two o'clock in the morning. Imaginary scorpions ran up and down my legs, hostile tribesmen snatched my beloved children. I desperately searched for a way out—without losing face, of course. There were many nights like that, lying in the darkness with my heart pounding as my imagination ran riot. Snakes—the country must be teeming with them. I sneaked quietly out of bed and into the bathroom, where at least I could sit and contemplate in light and reality.

After that followed a long think-out period during the summer holidays. Our decision if and when to go was governed by many important factors. The experts and climatic charts informed us that the ideal time to arrive in Central Africa was February-March, during the dry season. Working backwards from this we had to allow plenty of time for our desert crossing. There was also the children's schooling to consider. By incorporating the Christmas holidays, we hoped to minimize the amount of time lost and planned to try and teach them ourselves on the trip. During October David was heavily committed with the Earls Court Motor Show and needed a further month to tidy up his business commitments and Susan and I had to give a reasonable period of notice to get leave of absence from our jobs. On October 1st we made our final decision to go, starting date December 1st.

An excited telephone call from Susan the next day telling us she had got leave of absence made our numbers up to six. She joined us for supper that evening and over steak and a bottle of wine we shouted each other down with suggestions, misgivings and a few bawdy jokes, but we were quite serious about the expedition. Our original plan had been greatly modified. We had proposed to sail to Lagos, as Susan and I refused to have anything to do with a Sahara crossing, and then drive through Central Africa to Kenya. After a reasonable rest we then planned to cross by boat to India and drive home. Following a few letters to shipping companies, we discovered it would cost $1,000 to sail to West Africa with our long wheelbase Land Rover and trailer, much more than we could afford. There was only one other way to get there, drive across the Sahara! Similarly, when we looked at the cost in outlay and lost earning time, we felt we must confine ourselves to Africa. India would have to wait until another time.

A few letters from David here and there brought us some rather premature publicity. As yet I had not told the children and when a photographer arrived one wet miserable Friday afternoon and busily clicked away with us all standing round the Land Rover I passed it off as part of a series on overland vehicles.

Susan and I spent an agonizing Saturday worrying about medical ethics, our bosses' reactions and going to work the following week. Next morning, there it was in a Sunday paper for all to see. The children read it in total disbelief and hysterical laughter, alternating between dashing round the kitchen hugging us all in turn and running back to the newspaper to read more. "You have got to be joking." said Peter. "What about Finnigan (our cat)?" asked Sean. "I cannot stay away from school that long." said Sarah with a troubled frown. But the more they read, the more excited they became. After a hectic breathless breakfast they all took off in different directions, only to return at ten minute intervals with more and more questions. "How much further is the Sahara than Sheerness?" "What do we do about going to the loo?" "Do we have to take any school books?" They really had no idea what the trip involved. We put up a map of Africa on the kitchen wall and drew in our proposed route. Europe looked so small, my heart started racing all over again.

Needless to say the telephone rang most of the day with offers of low mileage camels and cracks about Dr. Livingstone from our highly amused friends. Each post for the next two weeks brought letters full of enthusiasm and encouragement. The kindness and willingness to help and advice by so many complete strangers was quite overwhelming. Only after some time did we realize that the press publicity had produced a mountain of valuable information.

After the initial excitement the hard work began. We compiled list after list—and then lists of lists, dividing the chores. The local library sent in a steady stream of all the books it could locate on the Sahara and Central Africa and we talked at great length to many long distance travellers and experts. David and Jeffrey already owned the right vehicle for our trip, a long wheelbase six cylinder petrol Land Rover. Jeffrey, a brilliant engineer, soon compiled a long list of necessary modifications and he and David designed a trailer to carry all our food and supplies. Food, medicines, clothes and paperwork were my department. It was not difficult, but very time consuming trying to organise everything and do a job as well. David worked late into the evening getting cars ready for the Motor Show and I dashed backwards and forwards to my surgeries, using every spare minute to fill in never ending forms.

The children hovered in a state of suppressed excitement. They had already travelled many miles with us since carry cot days, all over Spain and Portugal, quick trips to France and Germany and one devastatingly expensive week in Austria. Our family sport was sailing and both boys were competent sailors, Peter qualifying for his first R.Y.A Certificate when he was only ten. The thought of our African expedition thrilled them, but I suspect that each one had a few quiet moments of doubt and apprehension especially when their school friends regaled them with glorious bloodthirsty tales of man-eating lions and hissing cobras. "I think I will sleep in the Land Rover," announced Sean, slinging his coat on the floor after school. "Why would you do that when there is a perfectly good bed upstairs?" I asked. "I mean when we go to Africa. There are bound to be animals and things and they are not going to get me!"

Sean was a sturdy well built ten year old with broad shoulders, unbelievable determination and the physical strength to see any situation through to the bitter end. In strange contrast, from a very early age he was always afraid of animals and "creepy crawlies"—until he got to know them when he would guard them with his life. Although English born, he was well-named and had inherited many delightful Irish traits from David. Music, poetry and painting were always more important than history and sums. His capacity, even as a small child, for deep emotional attachment and affection always endeared this different one of our brood to our hearts, even when his will and ours were locked in headlong conflict. Blonde and slim, Peter at 12 and Sarah, only 8 when we left England, were two of a kind. Gentler by nature, they expressed their likes and dislikes in a less forceful manner. Peter planted his feet firmly in David's footsteps each day, always ready to take over the care and protection of the family in his father's absence. Eager to learn as much as possible about engineering, he proved a great asset and companion for David during the trip and could hold a mature conversation with any man about Land Rover problems.

"Show me a mountain and we will climb to the top" David had told me as he courted me romantically some 15 years previously—me a penniless medical student, David in his first job after National Service. "Do you see that star?" he pointed over Edinburgh as we stood on the low grassy slopes of the Pentlands. "It is going to be ours." Well, here we are, many happy hard working years behind us, a solid foundation laid, ready to step off the world's gang plank and swim to new horizons.

"I am going to be sick." whispered Sarah Jane as the Wimpy bar door slammed behind us. I scooped her up and rushed for the gutter. An hour previously we had had the first series of our battery of immunizations for tropical travellers. We all felt rather seedy and compared the sizes of our swelling, throbbing arms as we made our way home. "I will buy you all a coke." said David to the children hoping to cheer them up. Sarah and Sean burst into tears, Peter sat in miserable silence. I did not know whether I wanted to cut off my arm or my head. We shivered and shook for two days and moaned through restless nights, but suddenly life was great again. "It will never be that bad again." I reassured everyone with my fingers crossed behind my back.

In the short, quiet hours, when all the children were at school I tried to come to grips with the formidable food list. Despite everyone's forebodings we were determined to take our trailer and carry as much food as possible. Dehydrated meals are light and compact but I felt they were neither adequate nor palatable in large quantities for my growing and gourmet family. Our telephone bill soared frantically as I tracked down suppliers of tinned bacon, butter and cheese. I spent days wandering round 'cash and carries' selecting tins of meat and pies. One kind London firm gave me a large supply of dried egg powder which proved invaluable in later weeks as a source of protein and added variety.

The days were never long enough nor the spare room large enough to accommodate the steadily growing pile of equipment and supplies. To add to my increasing state of nervous tension, David's public relations man had arranged a press conference in London, more newspaper interviews and worse still a couple of radio interviews. Listening to these afterwards I sounded like a breathless neurotic—perhaps that is how I would end up.

Two days before we were due to leave, having burnt the midnight oil checking and packing our gear, we dressed up for a quiet theatre date with Jeffrey. As we walked in through his front door to pick him up, two silent figures, dressed in flowing white Arab robes, glided down the stairs. Elegant beaded and veiled ladies lounged on the sofa. Shrieks of laughter echoed through the house as more and more friends appeared in their empire builders' gear and leopard skin loin cloths. In the middle of the dining room table sat a beautiful cake in the shape of a Land Rover. It was quite a night and a wonderful surprise party.

On December 2nd we left home fully laden amidst smiles and tears from our friends who had gathered to see us off. For David and myself there was a feeling of great relief. The weeks of planning and packing were all but over. Ahead lay a 36 hour respite on the boat to Spain before the long drive would begin. As David so rightly said, we had been doing 'ten-tenths' for weeks and we lapsed into an almost drug-like induced state of relaxation on the boat. A handsome tip at Southampton had ensured that we were last on—and first off at Bilbao! Customs paled at the sight of all our gear so early in the morning and after a cursory glance waved us on. The sun shone, the air was warm and we all looked forward to our long journey with enthusiasm.

It was many years since we had driven along those same roads with the children, then they were very young and quite a handful during the long hours. This time we could share our delight with them as we climbed over the mountains and wound our way through tiny Spanish villages. We pleaded the need for five minutes peace and David slipped Grieg's Peer Gynt Suite into the cassette player. The children listened in silence to the beautiful simple musical. "Just imagine." I whispered, as they captured the magic, "Just imagine us digging out the sand, working faster and faster, puffing, panting, then that wonderful, wonderful moment as the truck pulls away and we roll peacefully along on the golden sands." We lived each note, everyone building a picture, a story, creating for themselves a musical journey across the Sahara. Although there were the usual traffic jams on the Bilbao road, we reached Madrid in the late afternoon and took the hotel plumbing system by storm. Even the children revelled in long hot baths and clean clothes.

Sarah sighed deeply as she patiently sat through a three hour Spanish lunch next day. David and the boys had escaped to shop and look round the beautiful city. "I had quite a problem dragging them out of the Prado." he explained that evening. "They were fascinated and would have stayed for hours."

The boys sat in silence, glowering at their father. We had a family crisis on our hands. "What?" I demanded. "What have you done to their hair?" They both looked like something out of a medieval history book—no, at least the fringes in those days were straight. The two before me had locks dipping over one eye and rising over the other in pained, surprised disbelief. "You did not actually pay for that?" I asked in despair. The boys stormed out in disgust and I followed with a bottle of shampoo and hairspray hoping to make amends. Peace was soon restored with David and the boys getting out all the hotel notepaper from the bureau and designing a new series of aeroplanes. Shortly thereafter, the telephone rang at the side of my bed, and clutching a towel I groped my way out of the shower. "Look out of the window" urged the desk clerk in rapid Spanish. A dark stain spread round my feet on the pale green carpet as the water trickled slowly down my calves. "Whatever for, what is the problem?" I asked him. "Just look, Señora, please look." he pleaded. I let the telephone fall onto the table with a clatter, dragged back the curtain and peered down into the street. The road, car tops and verandas opposite were all littered with paper aeroplanes! I turned back to the telephone. "I am sorry. Very sorry. I will stop it at once." I assured him. Still clutching my inadequate towel, I rushed next door, just in time to see David launch his new supersonic model out of the window.

"Hold my hand, tell me what to say, don't leave me." I pleaded in the early hours of Friday morning. David's Spanish friends had organised yet another press conference and I dreaded the thought of answering all those questions in another language. "You are the one who speaks Spanish." David reassured me. "You will have to help us out." I smudged my eye shadow, wiped it off and started again. I thought it was just us and the desert now. I could not remember the verb 'to hope'. As Sean entertained the maids in the corridor, strumming his guitar and singing them a love song, Sarah and Peter scrambled around on their hands and knees searching for odd socks and dirty underpants under the beds. David buttered and jammed all the extra rolls on the breakfast trays and stuffed them into my day bag for the journey. At last we were ready. The reporters and newsmen greeted us with the charm and courtesy we had grown to love in Spain. With their natural and endearing affection for children, they quickly overcame any language barriers, gathered vast amounts of information and sent us on our way with smiles and happy memories of Madrid.

With only a few hours of daylight left, we drove non-stop to Jaen to find the Parador closed for the winter. Then began the first of many hotel hunts. After a good night, though, and a lazy start to the morning, we were still undecided whether to make it a short day and stay in Granada or press on. Finding the new motorway to Malaga decided the issue; we had not been looking forward to the mountain roads at dusk and were delighted to find a good fast road.

It was dark when we arrived in Malaga but we soon found the camp site with the help of a friendly policeman; then the fun began. We had never camped before, although we did have a practice run at putting up the tent in the garden before we left, just to make sure we could. We even colour-coded the various bits of the frame. None of this helped in the dark. Sarah sat on the bonnet of the Land Rover and timed us. One hour and twenty minutes later we were partly organised although Sean and I were still fighting with one of the camp beds. Peter watched with an amused smile until he could stand it no longer and clicked it all together in 30 seconds, much to my disgust.

Our first night camping was a great success except that Sean insisted on rescuing a small black and white cat from the prowling dogs. There were six of us in the tent all night, one with more than their fair share of fleas! At 6 a.m., Sarah slid down to one end of her camp bed which then automatically folded up and she was quickly propelled through the air into the side of the tent. We all shook with laughter as Peter dragged the squeaking bundle back on to her bed but Sarah was not amused. The strange behaviour of our heavily elasticated camp beds was to provide a lot of laughter for 8,000 miles. Nothing reduced our family to tears of merriment quicker than the sight of Mummy accidently sitting on the end of her camp bed, the sudden snap as the other end folded up and the cry of despair that followed.

Daylight in Malaga showed us that we were only about 80 feet from the edge of the sea in a large eucalyptus grove. We set about tidying up our camp site while the boys played ping-pong on the trailer lid which was also constructed as a large table. Hot coffee, bacon and fried bread got everyone off to a good start for the day and Sarah remembered to do the rounds with the anti-malarial tablets. The boys did their all-important daily Land Rover and trailer check. It would prove to be a most worth-while thing to do.

We spent two days and three nights in Malaga listening to more and more horror tales from fellow campers of how they had been attacked and robbed in Algeria and Morocco. One large group—all set to cross the desert—had turned back thoroughly disillusioned and dis-heartened. My heart sank—what were we letting ourselves in for? David and Peter spent half a day devising further alarm systems for the Land Rover. We had already fitted the equipment which set off the horn if the doors were opened but most of our gear was packed on the roof and in the trailer, and these were totally unprotected. With spools of wire, blocks of wood and dead matches, David rigged up a much more extensive alarm system. On Tuesday morning we got up early and packed up camp.

Susan had been unable to start the journey with us after a quick medical check up showed that she needed to have her gall bladder out. She planned to convalesce and fly out to Nigeria and join us there. Ten days before we were due to leave England the telephone rang. "I'm coming" a determined voice told me over the crackling wires from Scotland. "I know you're coming Susie, your ticket to Nigeria should be on the way to you in the next few days." "But I don't want to fly to Nigeria. I don't want to miss the Sahara crossing." "You're not serious darling; you only came out of hospital yesterday. You must have been drinking." "Only the one" she laughed. "If I meet you in North Africa it will be three weeks after my operation. I'm sure I can make it. If there are going to be any complications, they will have happened by then and I will send a telegram." I didn't know what to say. "I'll have a chat with David—and telephone you back. Meanwhile you had better start your press-ups." I put the kettle on for a cup of coffee. By all accounts crossing the desert would be a rugged journey. We already had the responsibility of three children now it looked as if we would have a convalescent patient as well. Tall and strong,

Susan had never been particularly athletic, always preferring to curl up in an armchair with a book. The first few days after her operation had left her shocked and depressed—the experience of being on the receiving end of the surgical knife for the first time had horrified her. I found it difficult to assess how quick a recovery she would make. When David came home for lunch, we turned over the possibilities and implications.

"I'll chance it if you will" he finally said "but you're the doctor, you'll have to cope if things go wrong." I blew him a kiss as his car spluttered and backfired down the road on his way back to work, then dialled the travel agents. "I want to cancel the ticket to Nigeria for Dr. Susan Cole and book one to Tangier." So here we were packing frantically and leaving Malaga in great haste to meet her plane. We arrived with time to spare in Algeciras for the ferry across to Ceuta. It was a dirty old boat but it took us to Africa, the children loved it.

CHAPTER 2

MOVE UP THE BED . . .

"NO GUNS, NO big guns, no little guns", David assured the officer as he poked his head through the Land Rover's window. Moroccan customs were slow and ponderous. They didn't seem interested in the bottles of cheap whisky we had bought with our remaining pesetas—only guns. Eventually they waved us through. It goes without saying that in our rush we forgot to put our watches back, so we arrived at Tangier Airport an hour too early. David went off with the children to find the local camp site and I waited for the plane. Late and anxiously looking for a familiar face Susan eventually struggled through the barrier weighed down with bags and straw hat. Catching sight of me her shoulders drooped even further and she burst into tears. Bundling her into a taxi, I listened to her unhappy tale of how her mother had fallen and broken her arm the previous morning just as she was leaving! Susan's last sight of her mother was as she was bundled into an ambulance in a blinding snow storm in the highlands of Scotland.

At least we hadn't had to take part in the tent saga that night, David and the children had it all organised for our arrival. Susan was welcomed with great delight by the children and settled in the reclining seat that David had fitted in the Land Rover, and spent a glorious exhibitionist half-hour showing off her gall stone and still very new scar to an admiring audience. After a large supper and celebration Scotch we all climbed thankfully into our sleeping bags. My silent doubts about starting the journey with a semi-invalid remained unvoiced.

Despite a blanket inside our sleeping bags, we froze during the night. In the morning the top of the tent was covered with a thin layer of ice and we were thankful to get up and stamp around. Sarah, last up as usual, left it too late—"I'm ruined, absolutely ruined" she cried as a puddle collected round her feet, but took in good part the laughter and vulgar taunt of "The phantom puddler strikes again" from the boys. It didn't take long for the sun to melt the frost and by 10.00am we were peeling off clothes and sun bathing. In the late afternoon Susan and I went into Tangier and strolled through the Souk. "Woolworths! Marks and Spencers! British Home Stores!" chanted the cheeky smiling young men offering their services as guides—a great advertisement for our major stores at home. One piece of shopping stretched our ingenuity somewhat. I was worried about the nightly wanderings of David and the boys to spend a penny. Not knowing what lay ahead, I felt it might be a little hazardous for them to stumble out of the tent half asleep into the dark African night. After much haggling over the price, I settled for three plastic milk churns with clip-on tops—'pee pots' as the boys christened them. We gazed longingly at the beautiful Kaftans, but resisted all attempts by the persistent shop keepers either to try or buy—we still had a long way to go.

All packed and anxious to get started on our adventure we headed for the Atlas Mountains. For two hours we drove along the edge of the Atlantic Ocean catching glimpses of white furling breakers and stretches of beautiful beach through the road-side trees. "Let's swim, let's swim" shouted the children enthusiastically, but we pressed on. Swerving to miss a group of men lopping the trees at the side of the road, the Land Rover suddenly felt heavy—even though we were not climbing. Going down to 3rd gear, it pulled to the right. All was not well. Clambering out we all stood in a forlorn group round the nearside trailer wheel. The tyre was badly cut and on closer inspection the inner tube was shredded. "Trust Mummy" said Peter as he dragged out the tool box and jacked up the trailer. I tried to make amends by cooking a large lunch while David changed the wheel and pored over the map looking for the next garage. Luck was with us. Bearing more south west and away from the ocean, we found a garage in the next small town. They had a new inner tube and for 60p did a quick repair on the tyre. It was the end of the school day and we were surrounded by shy giggling children who stroked the Land Rover and politely greeted us in French. Relatively happy once more we headed off into the foothills of the Atlas Mountains, climbing steadily through bare brown terrain with attractive but poverty-stricken villages clinging to the slopes. Small donkeys carrying huge loads plodded patiently by their owners riding side saddle and kicking them monotonously on the neck. Each farm was a collection of small mud huts, distinguishable from the neatly stacked mud-plastered haystacks by their roofs held down by stones. Only the women—dressed in attractive blue and turquoise dresses and veils—gave a splash of colour to the otherwise drab countryside.

Tired and hungry we arrived in Sefrou after dark, but thankfully David had 'phoned ahead and booked us into a small hotel. French cooking and warm beds ensured a good night's rest and we delighted in the clear crisp mountain air and pretty village next morning. Veiled women sat busily weaving by hand and men carved shapes and figures with expert care. Susan sought out the post office—this was to become her obsession throughout the entire trip, and David took the boys to a local orphanage to deliver boxes of food and clothes from an English Church.

Packed and loaded with fresh bread and small sweet tangerines, we made a late start climbing higher and higher into the Atlas Mountains, through coniferous forests and up still more to bare round hills with distant jagged snow-streaked peaks. We estimated our height to be 9000ft. as we shivered despite anoraks, and quickly packed up the lunch things. Camping for the children was out of the question in such low temperatures and we decided to drive on and find more permanent shelter for the night.

Darkness came quickly and suddenly. We drove into Ksar-Es-Souk at about 8 p.m. but it felt like midnight. It looked black, menacing and unfriendly, we all felt very apprehensive about our first night in an Arab town. Winding in and out of the dark sandy streets we spotted a little bar full of locals and soldiers drinking coke. We had found our first "half-star" hotel. They had rooms above the bar with two double beds in one, and a large single in the other—all fairly basic but adequate. As there was only one threadbare blanket per bed we unpacked our sleeping bags but even then half the company slept in their clothes as the windows were merely slits, open to the cold night air. Sarah had trouble coping with the French type loo but a pair of dry trousers brought back her smile and we sat huddled together while the children embarked on one of their many 'medical chats' plying Susan with questions about caesarean sections and breech deliveries.

We were very worried about the Land Rover and all our gear on the roof. David parked it opposite our bedroom window and in addition to organizing a guardian for the night, he and Peter rigged up a secondary alarm system which would blow the horn if anyone even lifted the corner of the roof rack or trailer cover. Even so I woke at 3 a.m. to find him peering anxiously out of the window. In the cold and dark of the early morning we prised everyone out of their beds. The sinister-looking guard of the night before greeted us with a smile and ushered us into the tiny kitchen. Grouped round his welcome wood fire we drank hot sweet coffee and gave him English cigarettes.

Driving out of the town in the grey morning light we found it had been transformed by the rising of the sun. The rich red sandstone of the houses and buildings, the colourful flowing robes of the early risers and friendly waves and shouts from the children made us want to linger.

The road so far had been good, tar seal all the way. Fifty miles after leaving Ksar-Es-Souk it changed abruptly. The colour code on the map called it 'Piste'—but it turned out to be rough corrugated demanding track with deep potholes and wadis for the unwary, flanked by flat stony countryside. We were horrified and all, except David, a little frightened by the constant crashing up and down and bangs on the head from loose objects flying around the Land Rover. Stopping at regular intervals to check round the Land Rover and stretch our legs we were dismayed to find that the trailer hitch had developed a marked bend and looked in danger of snapping completely. Topping the next rise the road petered out; the broken bridge had been swept aside by the fast flowing stream. On the opposite side the bank rose virtually vertically for four feet. Although icy cold, the water was quite shallow and we nursed the Land Rover and precious trailer through, sweeping round the next hillside only to be stopped once more by a military road check at the village ahead. It was easier getting into the village than getting out. We wound our way through a maze of narrow streets, laughing children pointing one way and wryly amused elders pointing the other. After three complete circuits we made it. We had obviously lightened their day and they waved enthusiastically as we headed off. Grey emptiness surrounded us. No sound, no movement outside the creaking and crashing of the Land Rover. Each brow of a hill revealed nothing more than another never-ending stretch of track ahead.

After such an early start we agreed to make camp about 3.30 p.m. and we pulled off the main track to choose a spot in the elbow of two small hills. Instead of putting up the large tent we quickly erected the awning at the side of the Land Rover. Peter worked non-stop for an hour on camp beds and sleeping bags and Sean collected large piles of dry scrubby bushes. Sarah scrambled up and down the stony hillside collecting pretty white flowers that looked like Edelweiss and we all congratulated ourselves on our excellent choice of camp site. After supper we sat round the camp fire singing and playing the boys' guitar before falling into bed; tired, unwashed and fully dressed, hot water bottle, blanket and all for the second night running.

The temperature dropped slowly but steadily. By midnight we were frozen and restless. I dragged Peter into my sleeping bag hoping to generate a bit of heat but to no avail, I continued to shake uncontrollably and sleep was impossible for two on one camp bed. By 4 a.m. we had all had enough and were glad to get up and strike camp. After hot cereals and coffee we carefully picked our way down the hillside in the darkness looking for the Piste. Groaning with cold and fatigue we crashed back onto the track once more and hung on in miserable silence, but as dawn broke a great cheer went up. We turned right onto a smooth tarred road—a time for celebration and we handed round the sweets.

Averaging 20 m.p.h., after closely missing three dark brown camels in the half light, we arrived at Bou-Afra—a small, poor village. The locals were already up and about and directed us first to the bread shop and then to the petrol pump. Chatting to an interested bystander, David found he owned the local café, a tiny dark room opening off the street. He served us with thick black sweet coffee and a smile. Peter tried manfully to drink it, but discreetly poured most of it into mine.

Topped up with petrol we drove off into the glare of the rising sun with the mountains looking like black cardboard cut-outs in silhouette. Huge holes seemed to appear in the hillsides and bridges grew and disappeared in the sky as the shimmering heat haze played tricks on us. Well satisfied with our early morning mileage and warm at last, we enjoyed a long break on the road-side outside the frontier town at Figuig. Despite major opposition from the children, I heated up some water and insisted that everyone scrubbed hands, face and teeth followed by a brush down before presenting ourselves at the customs post. It was forbidden to take Moroccan currency out of the country, so Sarah and I rummaged through the contents of the tiny village shop while Susan and David filled in umpteen forms and declarations. When all were complete we were told to present ourselves at the next office round the corner and watched in silent amazement while the same official dashed around ahead of us, quickly buttoning on a greatcoat and with a serious face, stood waiting. Thinking we had now completed our exit from Morocco we relaxed and drove off through a stretch of sand dunes and palm trees only to be confronted by a wooden barrier and a somewhat scruffy looking official in a tent. He made the position quite clear. For two packets of cigarettes he would lift the barrier, the alternative was a complete search of all our luggage. The Algerian officials were smart and extremely polite. I did not wait to be asked this time however, and handed out cigarettes as we arrived. They had a friendly chat with the children and gave us some advice on the road conditions ahead as they stamped our passports and carnet.

On a good fast road, we reached our next main stop Colomb-Bechar in daylight, giving us time to look around for a camp site. While David and the children explored the possibilities, Susan and I sat wearily in the Land Rover drawing curious stares from the passers by. The women were heavily veiled, observing us through a tiny triangular opening as they walked dutifully behind their husbands. I felt rather brash with my unruly hair and grubby jeans. The only place to camp with any safety, we were told, was on the dirt patch next to the police station. It was also a lorry park, dog's playground and public urinal. The ground was fouled and stank, and it was too hard to drive in a tent peg. The nearest toilets were down the road in a cafe and the only source of water was the police tap which ran for two hours in the morning while they washed their cars!

By carefully placing the tent, trailer and windbreak we managed to establish a small semi-private compound although keeping the low-hanging washing out of our coffee later proved a bit of a problem. The children were ready for an early bed and leaving Susan to baby sit, David and I wandered off round the town in the early evening in the hope of finding a laundrette. Ten minutes after we left, three friendly young French overlanders strolled across to chat to Susan and inspect the Land Rover, walking into one of our trip wires as they approached the camp and thereby triggering off the alarm. There was Susan panic-stricken, the vehicle locked up, the keys in David's pocket and the horn sounding off in the still night. No police appeared, of course, so Susan poured herself another whisky and hid in the tent! When the French boys could stand it no longer, they jerked out a piece of wire at the back of the Land Rover. They stopped the alarm, but in so doing short-circuited our electrics and the next morning the battery was flat!

The pee pots came into their own! Susan and I became quite expert but Sarah had aim problems and I had to pop into the town and buy her a small bucket. David managed to find a small garage with welding equipment and spent most of the next day lying on his back under the vehicle taking out the petrol tank so that he could remove the tow hitch, modify it and replace it. Meanwhile Susan and I set about the washing. Two soaks, a wash and a rinse left the final water only marginally less grey than the first but it was the best we could do. Appalled by the filth and flies we scrubbed all our cooking utensils and table plus everyones' hands with disinfectant but all in vain. The children developed acute abdominal pain and diarrhoea and we had to resort to 'bucket and chuck it'', as they say in the sailing world, burning everything we could with petrol in a deep pit.

As a special treat, but at a very high price, David organised hot showers for everyone in the local hotel. Restless and sickened by our dirty camp site we thankfully packed up our gear and after a full

Land Rover service, headed off in the late morning, driving for the first few miles past stinking rubbish dumps. The road was excellent, straight and flat through our first desert looking countryside, grey brown shale and scrubby bushes gave way to soft sand and scattered groups of palm trees. We saw browsing camels and small camps of nomads squatting in low brown tents and the children were sure that the Sahara was just around the corner. Although there were many signs saying 'Danger—Sable' there was no sand on the road and we pushed on late into the night arriving in Timimoun. A large board advertising the hotel Oasis Rouge described it as tourist class, which sounded like us, but finding it in the silent sleeping town was more difficult than we first imagined. "It's there, it's there," shouted Peter when we'd almost given up hope and we thankfully pulled up outside the impressive looking building. We hammered on the huge door for about five minutes, the children wide awake again and running around excitedly. A sullen youth peered out rubbing sleep from his eyes and reluctantly admitted there were plenty of rooms. We stepped into the large stone-floored hall. High ceilings and beautifully carved red sandstone walls gave it a church-like atmosphere and we dropped our voices to a hoarse whisper. The rooms were excellent although I suspected the sheets were on their second time round but nobody cared as we were all exhausted.

Stepping out into the wide corridor to look for the bathroom, I yelled with fright as a door quickly opened behind me and a hand grabbed my arm. A short elderly Arab dressed only in his white long john underwear spoke excitedly and volubly in French. "Yes, I am English. Yes they are my children, but where is the bathroom"? I asked. "Ah" he replied and with one hand firmly clamped on my bottom he propelled me along a long dark passage. "Voila" he exclaimed with a royal gesture pushing open a rickety old door. Despite my profuse thanks he seemed reluctant to leave so firmly pushing him out I wedged my foot against the door since the handle and lock were long since broken. Afterwards, as I peeped cautiously out, the white gnome-like figure sprang out of the shadows and with his bare feet pattering on the stone floor, duly escorted me back with hearty invitations to visit him in his room. Laughingly, I gave him half a packet of cigarettes, returned his friendly squeeze and promised to see him in the morning.

To our dismay we awoke to overcast skies and cold driving rain, there was nothing to do but keep driving. We climbed gradually up to the Plateau du Tademait which looked like the most godforsaken place on earth, 200 miles of totally flat featureless black slate with a ribbon of tarmac winding on for ever. The bleakness and loneliness silenced our normally chatty group and no-one lingered for more than a few minutes in the biting wind when we stopped each hour to change seats and drivers.

"Anyone feel like a Wimpy" grinned David, as we flashed past a crudely painted metal sign saying 'Cafeteria' seeing an Arab huddled in a blanket standing hopefully by the door of a tiny mud hut. I don't think it can have been a very profitable business as we didn't see another soul all day.

There had obviously been a lot of road works in progress since our map was printed. The Piste we dreaded never materialized and we made good time on tarmac roads, only pausing briefly for snacks and to refill the thermos with coffee. We decided to try the rest house at In Salah and save the agony of unpacking all our camping gear. Although still quite early in the evening, the town was dark and deserted as usual. Stopping at a little café for directions we found the Patron, a charming young man, fluent in French and eager to help. Jumping into the Land Rover beside me, he offered to show us the Rest House and we wound round tiny back streets to the market place. After long negotiations there in local dialect, he assured me that the room would be ready in 20 minutes if we would all return to his cafe and have a coffee. Before pulling away, I suggested that I should have a quick look at the room and he took me through a tiny doorway into a narrow passage. A huge boulder on the end of a piece of rope acting as a pulley rose above my head as he opened the next door. Peering into the gloom I could just make out an 'L' shaped room. On the mud floor on bits of sacking and wrapped in their robes lay about 20 Arabs, huddled together for warmth. "It will only take a few minutes to persuade them to move up and make you a place" explained my host kindly. Stooping low, I backed out through the doorway shaking my head at the expectant faces in the Land Rover. "It seems so much trouble, I think we'll just camp if there's anywhere nearby", I suggested. "No problem, I own a campsite 2km down the road" beamed the young man and leapt back into the front seat, and off we went. Swinging right, the truck suddenly slewed to the side, wheels spinning in the soft sand. It was a case of 'everybody out' and push into the campsite. In the light of the headlamps we saw tiny huts made out of palm branches and all around high dunes of golden sand. Sean's visions of one gigantic sand pit to play in had come true at last. It was difficult getting any help from the children to set up camp that night. They rolled and jumped and dug in the sand shrieking and yelling with delight and letting off steam after such a long miserable day.

Before bedding down we returned to the café where Le Patron served up hot soup and what he assured me was beef steak. I was too tired to eat and could not help thinking about the scraggy camels I had seen round the back as my knife refused to cut the tough meat. To my shame, I wrapped mine in a tissue and slipped it into my anorak pocket when Le Patron was in the kitchen, repeating the operation for Peter when David was looking the other way. The village dogs were well fed next morning!

With Susan and the three children safely tucked up in a little hut, David and I slept out under the awning having been warned about thieving and after dark visitors. Sleep came quickly, but not for long. A piercing scream from Sean jerked me awake, and I leapt out of my sleeping bag and into the hut all in one movement, cursing as I fell over the guy rope and folding chair across the doorway. No snakes, no scorpion, no glinting knife in his back! Just one miserable mosquito had bitten him on the face! But he refused to be placated, being quite sure by now that the hut was full of nasty flying things. Admittedly there were quite a lot of rather large beetles and creepy crawlies which I hadn't bothered to point out, so I crossly agreed that he could sleep in the Land Rover, or none of us would have got any sleep. David made him up a bed and at 3 a.m., now well and truly frozen, we crawled back into our sleeping bags only to be woken intermittently by the banging Land Rover door as Sean leaned out to spend a penny. We were all cross and tired in the morning and Sean's popularity had reached an all time low but hot coffee and rolls in the café soon revived us. Our charming friend refused all efforts to tip him but gave us his card to pass on to our friends in case they passed that way.

Police clearance was necessary before leaving for Tamanrasset—part of the clocking in and out system operated across the more hazardous stretches. They warned us of a bad section of track ahead. At the petrol station we met an international group of hitchhikers looking for a ride and a delightful Italian family in a short wheel based Land Rover. They had done the trip before, though, and set off confidently ahead of us. The first few miles presented no problems and I bowled along happily at the wheel. Quite suddenly I saw fountains of sand spurting up from the wheels of the Italians' truck and it swung in all directions. Chicken-hearted, I stopped and David took over. We hung on for dear life as the truck wallowed and pitched with David spinning the wheel this way and that. Susan grabbed the knees of the children on either side of her and they screamed with pain as her fingers dug in harder and harder. We laughed hysterically and shouted at the truck, urging it on as if it were a horse. As abruptly as it started, the soft sand section finished. We found ourselves on the dreaded corrugations which shook us and the truck to near death. Firmly strapped in, with all loose objects tightly wedged under the seats and stuffed into bags, we crashed up and down. Trying to outwit the cruel ruts, David put his foot flat down on the throttle searching for the optimum cruising speed at which our spring rates would best suit the corrugations. We estimated this to be 50-55 m.p.h. After watching the experienced Arab trans-Saharan lorry drivers, at this speed we should have floated over the top of the corrugations as the frequency of our suspension fitted in exactly with the valleys and ridges. Unhappily our heavily-laden Land Rover simply didn't have the power to get to that speed and hold it. At the other end of the scale, we had a worst possible speed of around 6-7 mph when we would have been better to have had the axles bolted directly onto the chassis and no springs at all. As we slowed down to this speed the spring rate acted against us in such a manner that the axles were being punched down straight on top of the next rut, producing desperate, prolonged shuddering in the vehicle. We went into what can only be described as limbo with the steering having no effect whatever and the vehicle drifting sideways and shaking from end to end before finally coming to a halt. Perhaps the trailer behind with different spring characteristics made the condition worse but there was nothing we could do except ride it out. After an hour that seemed like four, we stopped to check for loose nuts and bolts and early signs of damage. The Italians were already in trouble. Pausing to pick up a camp bed which had slipped off their roof, they found they had lost two roof rack clips and the whole thing was loose and in danger of falling off. We left them busily tying it all together with rope.

The children organised a wood patrol to spot any scraps which had literally fallen off a lorry. The romance of a camp fire under the stars had not been dulled by our miserable cold nights. As they needed a chance to have a long play in the sand we stopped early, with only 85 miles on the clock for the day, we pulled well off the Piste in case we were mown down in the night by long distance lorries. Now that we had more or less mastered the art of keeping warm at night, we just put up the awning and then relaxed under the dying sun, while the children ran up and down the low hillsides and flew their kite.

Susan by this stage had made a fantastic recovery from her operation and was able to help more and more with the laborious chore of packing and unpacking all our gear. An early and breezy riser she would whip us into life, grabbing our cosy sleeping bags almost before we had time to get out. Sarah and I were never nice about it, belonging to the 'slow starter—strong finisher' brigade, but Susan's efforts were invaluable and greatly relieved the work load for David and myself. The boys learnt more and more about the Land Rover and helped David to check and service it at every opportunity, while Sarah accepted all situations with humour and her usual tranquillity. We had really settled down as a very happy team. Despite the long hours on the road, the children were never bored. They either organised their own games or we made up quizzes or listened to music on tape. Susan read aloud to them when they needed quiet time and for hours on end they would retreat into a world of fantasy and make-believe, designing new trucks and trailers and desert assault courses for action men.

David's concern about the Land Rover became an obsession. It was our lifeline and the whole success of our trip depended on its continued good running and maintenance. Our specially-built trailer with Land Rover wheels and no brakes had so far given us no cause for worry once David had modified the tow hitch, but this extra ½ ton was an added strain to our already heavily-laden truck. To enable us to carry enough petrol for the very long stretches David had built in an extra 20 gallon tank along one side in the back. The two tanks plus jerry cans round the side of the trailer and front of the Land Rover gave us a theoretical 800 miles range, assuming 10 m.p.g. Our seven large polythene water carriers were carried well forward on the roof rack to help balance the axle loadings, and our tent, camp beds etc., each had their allotted slot. We had allowed only one sail bag per person for personal clothes and possessions and added one suitcase containing a respectable set of clothes for each of us when the occasion demanded. A 'fair estimation' run and 'accurate weigh-in' before we left were all shelved in the delivery and fitting of equipment. Susan and I soon accepted that our most frequent view of David and the boys for three months would be 'bottoms up, heads buried' under the bonnet or with feet poking out from underneath the Land Rover.

Blank to provide start of next chapter on recto page

CHAPTER 3

PICKLES FOR SALE . . .

ONLY 350 MILES to Tamanrasset. Dawn broke in all its glory on the Saharan hillside. Mile after mile of golden sand surrounded us. The desert of the picture books stretched in all directions. A tremendous feeling of happiness and freedom gripped us all and in high spirits we clambered aboard ready for a new day. Five minutes later laughter turned to groans as we crashed back onto corrugated Piste. What had seemed simply like a nightmare was in act a reality. Seat belts firmly fastened, we braced ourselves once more and hung on to the seat backs and the dashboard. It did not take David long to adopt the method of many small truck trans-Saharan drivers. Whenever possible he peeled off the Piste, weaving and tacking in the smoother but often very soft ground on either side. With one eye on the compass and the other straining against the bright light to keep sight of the cairns marking the Piste, Susan and I broke our rule about not smoking inside the Land Rover and lit up with shaking hands and pounding hearts. A sudden lurch with an unnerving wallow from side to side threw up a thick blanket of sand which obscured all our vision and poured in through every tiny crack, leaving us all gasping and coughing. That was the signal for a very low gear, foot flat down and head back for the Piste.

In the late morning it was my turn to drive. Hat set, hands firmly clamped on the gyrating wheel, I stuck doggedly to the Piste for the first half hour or so. Developing a bit more dash as I gained confidence however, I started nipping off to the left and right seeking smoother ground and a less traumatic ride for everyone. It was a baptism of fire. Everywhere I went it was soft sand and with non-stop shouting and instructions from the entire family I would have to head back to the Piste, only to be tempted a few minutes later by another set of tracks going off at an angle. Where one particular lorry ever went to I will never know. The tracks disappeared abruptly, my wheels spun and the engine screamed and we were well and truly stuck. "Mummy's done it again" yelled the children.

"First puncture, now first bog in", as we all got out to survey the scene. I was mortified as everyone looked at me with obvious disgust; it was definitely a case of sand ladders and shovels. We dug deep channels in front of the wheels and wedged the ladders in place. At a shout from David we pushed like mad and away he went only to grind to a halt 10 seconds later. After the second attempt, though, he was away, not stopping for us but heading back to the Piste. We trudged behind dragging the ladders, the children making great sport out of my miserable driving ability.

As lunch time approached, the scenery changed; small scrubby plants grew here and there and even the occasional anaemic looking tree. Grey slate stained the golden carpet and in the distance rose the first rocky outcrops of the Ahaggar Range. Driving along a narrow track as we entered the Gorge of Arak, high rock on either side, something glinted on the road-side ahead—it was another roof rack clip off the Italian truck. We decided to wrap it up and give it to them for Christmas in Tamanrasset! Everyone was hungry so we pulled into the shade of the overhanging hillside for a cook-up. Sliding off the top of the 'hump' as we had now christened the trailer, Susan and I were horrified by the sight before us. Pickle, peanut butter, cream cheese and my precious Christmas pudding were all floating free—liberally mixed with dust and sand and plastered over everything! Cooking oil dripped steadily into the sand through the bottom of the trailer. It was a disgusting mess. Hundreds of flies appeared from nowhere settling on our eyes and mouths as we tried to scrape and wipe up the revolting mixture. Meanwhile David fought with the petrol cooker which could still reduce us all to a state of bad language and bad temper. It either refused to light or blew out in the wind. Our initial timidity at lighting it had long since disappeared. Once the burners were hot the petrol vaporized as we tried to prime it, so there was nothing to light in the little cups. We soon developed the technique of priming from a separate small tin with a fine nozzle and regular results—the whole cooker would momentarily go up in flames with a roar and everyone frantically kicked sand round it, but at least 9 times out of 10 it worked. Peter quickly became the cooker expert and at every stop it was his first chore to get it going and put on the kettle.

After a large meal we surveyed the trailer situation once more. Fortunately most of our food was packed in very large plastic boxes with lids firmly tied. Very little was loose and free to move around. I wedged the three remaining intact one gallon tins of oil on a foam base and closely packed in the damaged articles. Despite repeated and loud protests from David, Susan and I stood firm—we refused to put back the remains of the large pot of pickle. The top was cracked and all the sticky tape in the world was no guarantee against repeated disasters. We had a similar catering size pot of Mango Chutney, as yet still intact, and we looked at it with some misgivings.

We finally drove off leaving the half gallon container of Pan Yan at the side of the track. We were to learn during the journey that the locals usually came and examined every scrap of garbage we left behind, even digging it up after our efforts to 'Keep Africa Tidy'! We could only hope that they liked pickles in that area! The track climbed steadily into the foothills of the Ahaggar Mountains, wind-scarred, flattened, red rock heights on either side preventing any escape from the appalling twisting corrugation and large boulders. Flattening out as we reached the plateau the greyish sand was broken by jagged hills and outcrops of slate and shale standing end up. We made very poor time in these conditions, only averaging 15 m.p.h., but wanting to make Tamanrasett (rapidly approaching the dimensions of heaven) next day, David drove until dark. Carefully weaving in and out the deep gullies and knife-edged slate we tucked into the side of a hill and the boys made a large camp fire with their good day's collection.

A hot meal and a few songs soon cheered us up again and we pored over the map in the firelight. We estimated that it was only 160 miles to Tamanrasett and with an early start and good luck, we should make it in one run.

Too tired to fight with camp beds, the children cleared the stones round the truck and we spread the thick plastic sleeping bag covers over on the ground and put up the awning. Wanting no part of this, the boys made themselves beds in the truck and were soon fast asleep. Susan had remembered reading in an article about an Arctic expedition that 8% of body heat is lost from the head area. So we added woolly hats to our unlikely looking bed time garb of pyjamas, jeans, sweaters and ski socks and found we slept reasonably well, except for David and I who did our hourly, though involuntary check-ups.

Howling wind dragged me back from dreams of steak and hot baths. Peering at my watch I groaned inwardly, it was only 1 a.m. The side of the awning bulged and flapped hitting me in the face, an icy blast whistled under the Land Rover. Everyone was still sleeping so I turned over, hoping for the best. Twenty minutes later the side of the awning took flight with a resounding snap, stretching horizontally over us. Sand and dust swirled in. David fought with his blanket which had knotted itself round his legs and struggled out grabbing a shovel. I clutched repeatedly at the flapping canvas, and dragging it vertical once more, hung on frantically while David buried the edge and piled up a large wall of sand and stones. Cursing as he stumbled over the sharp slate rocks, he reinforced all our edges before struggling and grunting his way back into his highly disorganised sleeping bag, but at least I got a kiss in the middle of the night!

Up at 5:30 a.m. and with much less packing to do we were rolling in an hour, our sights set on Tamanrasset. Stopping as usual for our hourly driver change and vehicle check, a shout from Peter sent us all rushing to the trailer. One of the heavy iron supports, used when the trailer was unhitched from the Land Rover, had gone, ripped clean off. On closer inspection we found that the hinges holding the trailer lid had snapped and we had to tie it down with a heavy strap. Worse was to come. A yelp from Sean doing his wheel checks sent us rushing round to the other end of the Land Rover. The front nearside hub was running very hot and leaking oil. From David's expression, Susan and I realized that this was serious and quickly set about making coffee and sandwiches. In times of anxiety or fatigue I had found it was very important to provide snacks and hot drinks to allay rising tension and restore flagging optimism.

With the compass needle on 'S' we drove on—even more determined to reach Tamanrasset. Within the hour our hopes dwindled. We slowed to pass one old white ambulance with a group of young people standing around it, drinking and smoking. They returned our waves, so we pressed on believing all was well with them. Five miles further on, we stopped seeing an old Bedford van parked a few hundred yards to the right of the track. It looked in a sorry state with water carriers, jerry cans and bedding stacked all around it. Richard, a young American had been stuck there for 4 days. Miriam, his English girl friend, had just returned after hitching a ride to Tamanrasset and back in search of a new battery. She had returned empty handed, the price was too high. It called for an immediate segregation of the sexes. Men and boys grouped around the van and its sick engine whilst girls and women brewed up tea and chattered incessantly about less important matters. It was lovely to talk to someone else in English, swap experiences and commiserate about the dust and the cold.

Swinging the Land Rover around near the Bedford, David got out the jump leads, hoping to feed life into the dead battery, but it soon became apparent that the problem was much more complicated. The desert had taken its toll on their battery and the plates had broken free inside the case. Likewise the positive and negative poles had fractured and become loose, producing very poor contact. At the same time they had a carburetion problem and despite the wind and dust, David had to stretch a towel out on the sand and strip the carburettor down to the smallest part only to find it had a perforated diaphragm. There was little he could do about that. After cleaning out the jets, two of which looked as if they had been blocked for a very long time, and reassembling all the parts, the engine started practically straight away. Although they were obviously not particularly happy, it would produce half its useful power and enough to get them to Tamanrasset with luck!

Richard was flabbergasted and delighted. The carburettor was a completely closed book to him—both before and after David had given him a crash course. Not carrying any spare parts or even an instruction manual, life was difficult when things went wrong.

Leaving Miriam quickly packing all their gear and Richard nursing the engine, we waved goodbye and wished them well. We had no sooner got under way than everyone complained they were hungry, so with only 20 more miles towards our target, we pulled off into the shade of a tired looking tree in an area of softish sand. Happily eating our corned beef mash we saw in the distance behind us a great cloud of dust approaching. To our delight it was Richard and Miriam. Working on the principle that once it is going the only thing to do is drive flat out, Richard was going like a madman, regardless of corrugation and pot holes and sometimes almost airborne. As they flashed past we all waved and shouted encouragement only to fall silent as they made a fast U-turn back to us, heading straight for the soft sand. Thinking we may have broken down, they were coming back to help. As their wheels spun and engine howled, speed dropping quickly to zero, we all ran forward shouting reassurance and pushing the almost stationary van. A great sigh of relief went up as they picked up speed again and continued south across the desert, trailing the inevitable dust cloud behind them.

We had lost any hope of making our target by now. The track was so rough and or average speed so low, the advantage of our early start was lost. Rounding the hillside an hour later, there were Richard and Miriam on the brow and we drew alongside. The Bedford engine was still running but it had no power. David diagnosed the problem as fuel starvation to the carburettor and showed Miriam how to drip feed it from a plastic bottle every time it coughed. This was a particularly hazardous operation as there was a high risk of explosion inside the vehicle if she poured petrol over the electrics or down the exhaust manifold instead of down the carburettor. Fortunately they travelled with both sliding doors in the fully open position which meant a fairly free flow of air through the van and reduced the risk somewhat. The Bedford, being a forward control vehicle, had the advantage that the engine was virtually sitting in the driving compartment between the driver and his partner which made drip feeding of the carburettor possible—but highly dangerous. Deaf to our warnings, this happy-go-lucky pair set off again, using a pair of Miriam's panties as a filter and 'chain' smoking in the petrol laden atmosphere, they had not a care in the world!

We overtook, feeling there was little else we could do and saw to our surprise a signpost to the right 'Proper Road Ahead'. With a tremendous cheer from us all, the Land Rover crashed up the ridge on to the tar seal and wound through the abandoned French Atomic Testing Station, a large ghost town of derelict buildings and wire fences. With mile after mile of tarred road and only the occasional pothole, the speedometer clicked round and we shared out the sweets to celebrate. Coming to the end of the complex and back onto corrugation we no longer cared—it was the final run into Tamanrasset.

CHAPTER 4

SANTA CAME BY CAMEL . . .

THE CAMPING D'ASSINE looked like paradise in the late afternoon sun. It was a large clean sandy compound surrounded by a 7 ft. high wall, small two-roomed bamboo huts grouped under the trees and flowers to make it look just like home. Tall proud Tuaregs in their beautiful peacock blue and white robes stood by the gate to welcome us and allocate us a hut and make sure we had everything we needed. On the right of the gate was 'Hotel d'Assine,' a slightly bigger hut where breakfast was served each morning, if you had an hour or two to spare, all included in the camping fee. We viewed the scene with great satisfaction and relief and decided there and then to stay put for a few days and take a well earned rest.

Parking the Land Rover close against the side of our hut we unpacked our grubby bits and pieces and inspected the bed situation in the rooms. Only two beds in each, so we dragged two camp beds off the roof and hired two more foam mattresses from the guardian—imagine it, a mattress to sleep on! We stretched out, just to test them and lay there unable to move. "There's two cold showers, a large stone sink and running tap and three disgusting loos" reported

Sean, face flushed with excitement then tore off to explore some more. What more could we want, we were all set for a happy Christmas.

Struggling to my feet half an hour later I half heartedly set about making some supper whilst Susan and David drifted around the camp chatting to the various groups of overlanders from many different countries. Rounding up the children to eat was difficult as they were so delighted to find other people to talk to and dashed from hut to hut chatting to anyone who would listen.

It was a weary group that eventually sat around the table picking at their food. We all needed a few good nights sleep and respite from the constant travelling. I scraped the half-eaten meals into the rubbish bin, stacked the dishes in a corner and announced bedtime, it was 7 p.m. We put the children in one room and Susan and I slept at one end of ours on bunk beds. Poor David had nothing but a camp bed and mattress beside the door, I think he must have felt lonely. "I am going to take up holy orders" he said zipping up his sleeping bag. We laughed and all fell asleep.

Next morning the sun split the skies. We stretched and lounged in the soothing heat, reluctant to start on the long list of chores. Then two sleepy figures emerged from the hut next door and greeted us with hugs and shouts. It was Richard and Miriam! Slowly but surely they had limped into Tamanrasset arriving long after we had gone to bed. We all sat around chattering and laughing and drinking coffee turning a blind eye to the unwashed dishes and crumpled beds. Eventually we had to face facts, every hour of the next few days had to be used to get us and our vehicle ready for the next more hazardous section of the Sahara.

We had all been in the same clothes night and day for at least 4 days—and the same pullovers for three weeks. Reluctantly children and adults alike were marched over to the icy cold showers, everyone fighting for last place in the queue. As each one emerged, shining and slightly breathless, they reassured the next in line with a sadistic grin that "once you got used to it you felt marvellous!" Looking around at our washed and freshly clothed group, we really did look well, with glowing weathered faces, only marred by slightly swollen chapped lips caused by the cold dry wind.

How I longed for my old Bendix when I saw the pile of dirty washing. It took Susan and I two hours of nonstop scrubbing on the stone wall next to the tap before we triumphantly tied up the clothes line and pegged out the first load. That called for a cup of coffee and a cigarette, anything to put off the evil moment of inspecting the trailer. When we finally mustered the energy and courage we slid off the lid, the only thing to do was to sit down and have another cigarette! All the gallon tins of cooking oil had burst and the contents mixed with thick dust had spread malignantly round all the tins and equipment on the floor of the trailer, soaking off labels and covering them with a tenacious slime. But that was not all. The tins from a whole carton of evaporated milk had broken loose and lodged themselves under the oil tins with the constant crashing up and down over the corrugations. The milk tins had been pounded to death, some bursting and adding sour milk to the gritty, sticky mixture. There was nothing else for it but to empty the entire trailer, wash everything and repack. Stopping to cook lunch, I announced with a flourish that it was steam pudding for afters. I had heated up two tins. The first one was chocolate but the second was to be a surprise as the label had come off—a surprise it was, ham! It was obviously no good guessing at the contents of the unlabelled tins, so Susan and I now had the added chore of coding them all from the numbers stamped on the end of each one. We carefully examined all the damaged milk tins, discarding any that were weeping or looked suspect. This was to be our downfall as we found to our cost in weeks to come. We should have given away all the damaged tins there and then and avoided the repeated explosions of sour milk through our supplies.

The gloom over the trailer did not dim the sunshine or the pleasure of having a fixed base for a few days. The children dragged us eagerly by the hand outside the campsite gates to see a large caravan of camels kneeling in the sand, heads held high with disdain. Assembled in a chattering group were a dozen young French people, newly arrived from Paris to spend 8 days on a camel safari in the desert. The scene quickly changed to farce as the prospective riders approached their camels. Thick lips drawn back, yellow teeth bared, the camels bellowed and snapped at the feet and legs of their nervous passengers. Clinging white fingered and white faced to the wooden saddles the group lurched into the air as the Tuaregs kicked and pulled the complaining animals. With high pitched laughter the young Frenchmen goaded and teased the last girl of the party, now standing well back amongst the highly amused overlanders. She was even more reluctant than her camel to begin the adventure. At long last they were ready for the 'off', goat skins filled with water, feed on the pack animals and shoes slung around their necks as they perched almost cross-legged, bare feet pressed against the necks of their camels. Fresh from the Parisian winter, we felt they looked ill prepared for the days ahead, let alone the bitterly cold nights. The brochure selling that as a Christmas holiday must have been a good one!

The camp was a fascinating selection of vehicles and people, some travelling north and others south. Exchange of information about routes, problems and supplies provided endless hours of conversation. Maps spread in the sand, cars jacked up, and lines of washing. Everywhere we looked, it was the same, but all hands paused and heads raised as a large bus growled into the centre of the compound, towing an equally large and impressive looking aluminium trailer. A petrol and water bowser followed close behind. We had heard that buses crossed the Sahara but this was no ordinary bus, it was a German 'rolling hotel.' The thirty German travellers, clean and immaculate, viewed us all from their high, richly upholstered seats with mixed disbelief and pity. Climbing down from their air conditioned bus, they stood around in groups whilst the highly skilled engineers and drivers unhitched the trailer and opened it up to reveal a compact kitchen and refrigeration unit and separate bunk bed compartments for each passenger. Speechless with admiration, the overlanders moved forward to inspect everything at closer quarters and looked longingly at the cans of chilled lager being handed around the German party. Ten minutes later there was an uproar, two of the Frauleins had inspected the toilet facilities and were haranguing the Arabs with Germanic thoroughness. There were three lavatories, of the footplate and hole in the ground variety, to cope with 70-80 people. Although normally much more hygienic than the British type loo for communal living, none of these flushed and were rarely cleaned. It was a brave man or woman who could face them early in the morning. We all benefitted from the arrival of the Germans. Out came the hoses and the whole ablutions block was washed several times a day during their stay.

David spent his day tinkering with Richard's van and tired of working, Susan and I strolled down the tree-lined main street of the town in search of cigarettes. There were the dark closed-in little shops we had grown accustomed to in Arab towns, mostly selling bits of hardware and lengths of cloth and of course tourist shops with silver and leather work but all ridiculously priced. We looked in vain for some fresh food, only finding a few dates and apricots. There had not been any meat for sale in the town for ten days we were told. The petrol station was also the general store and cigarette shop and we bought a packet of an unknown brand to try them as everything else was sold out. It looked like being a lean Christmas with no cigarettes, no beer or wine of course in a Muslim community. David had been sleeping much better on his foam mattress at the camp so we decided to buy one for him as a combined Christmas and birthday present. "Only £12 Monsieur, a very good quality" coaxed the shopkeeper. "That is much too expensive" I replied backing out of the shop. "For you £9, Monsieur." "£5" I said entering into the spirit of the game. He spread his hands and shook his head sadly. "All right, £6." I conceded, counting the money out onto the counter. He smiled picked up the notes and shook me politely by the hand. Why do they keep calling me Monsieur? I asked Susan as we walked out into the bright sunlight. 'I don't know" she said. "Perhaps it's your short hair and trousers, come to think of it we haven't seen any Arab women in the streets at all." I got the feeling that the Arabs did not think much of the European women strolling around in masculine clothes and to be honest we did look a motley bunch.

Christmas Eve was a festival day for the Tuaregs and everything was closed and deserted. The children danced hopefully around the camp gates very early in the morning looking for the three small camels we had booked to take them for a ride but they never materialized. David turned his face to the wall and dozed while Susan and I sat impatiently in the Hotel d' Assine for over an hour longing for a hot drink. The harassed Arabs scurried to and fro first running out of milk then bread and finally coffee. A cold wind whistled through the gaps in the bamboo walls and the grey sky held no promise of better to come. With a gesture of despair, I scraped back my chair and marched off back to the hut to begin the long fight with the petrol stove. When the kettle started to sing I went quietly into the hut and sat on the edge of David's bed. Always an early riser, I knew there was more than fatigue making him reluctant to face the day. I smoothed the lines round his tired eyes. There was little I could do to relieve his burden of responsibility in carting a group of women and children across the desert and even less about the fact that we were never alone not even for five minutes. Communal living was proving more of a strain than we had anticipated; doubts, fears and personal chitchat remained unsaid. A slight movement near the door made me jump to my feet. We never got used to the silent Arab cleaners who wandered into the hut noiselessly and unannounced. With a shrug I went outside and made the coffee.

Richard had heard a rumour that there might be cigarettes in town perhaps at the little hotel. We all pooled and divided up what remained of our local currency. Susan and Miriam went off like addicts keeping a rendezvous with a 'pusher' whilst Peter brushed the sand out of the Land Rover and David spread out his tools ready for work. The trailer stood half empty so there was no doubt how I was going to fill in the day. Sean and Sarah hovered around Richard, fascinated by his bracelets and necklaces and constant good humour as he set about taking his engine to pieces. "Ask Richard if we can borrow his jack" David called to Peter, suddenly apprehensive about the soft ground as he slipped off our troublesome front wheel. "We will use it as a back up to our own." Peter reappeared waving it two minutes later. "Sean, slide underneath and put it in place, just to be sure" said David. Sean wriggled underneath the Land Rover in the soft sand, jack in hand. "Where shall I put it Dad"? Suddenly there was a creaking groan, a shudder from the Land Rover and a muffled shout from Sean. I flung myself to the ground grovelling in the sand. "Get him out man" yelled Richard running over. Spitting sand as I burrowed like a desert rat, I pulled out a white faced, whimpering little boy, feet first, hands tightly clasped round his chest. Swallowing hard to fight off the rising nausea, I dragged aside his hands and ripped open his shirt, my heart and Sean's thumping in unison. I carefully felt each rib in turn and then his abdomen. There was no major damage, just bruising and shock. Pale and tight lipped, David carried him round to the back of the hut and put him on my knee. As I rocked him in my arms and kissed away his tears, I sent up a silent prayer of thanks. "Peter come with me" said David quietly, "we've got to find something to use as a firm base for the jack, once is too often."

They returned carrying a solid square sheet of metal and slipped it in place. Stripping down the hub which had been overheating

David discovered that the gasket was fractured. That was one spare part we were not carrying. "Where's the children's toy bag?" he asked. I pointed to it on top of the trailer. Rummaging through the toy cars and games he selected a cardboard lid off one of the boxes. He laid it on top of the hub casting and tapped gently with a hammer for about ten minutes, finally sitting back with a satisfied grunt and holding up a new gasket. Peter helped to reassemble the hub and refit the wheel whilst David examined our other mechanical problems. We had early symptoms of gearbox seal failure, there was more oil in one box than there should have been. There was not much he could do about it except keep an eye on it and top up with oil whenever necessary.

After lunch the children and David went off in the Land Rover to test the front wheel and meet the prearranged guide who was going to take them to see some rock paintings. It was a highly unsuccessful outing. When they arrived at the little tourist office, the boss glanced around a group of youths lounging outside and signalled to one to get into the Land Rover. The young lad had no idea where he was going and pointed wildly this way and that in the desert finally leading them into an area of very soft sand. David was furious as Peter had to leap out to lock the free-wheeling hubs, everybody having to push to get rolling again.

Driving back into town thoroughly disgusted, they saw 3 or 4 vehicles parked together on the outskirts. One was the white ambulance we had passed in the desert and another was the French boys we had met in Colomb-Bechar. The children were highly excited, they always formed great attachments with any group we met and would look out hopefully for days in case we caught sight of them again. There were two girls and three young men in the ambulance—an English group. They had been stranded for five days out in the desert with radiator trouble and had finally run out of petrol on the last stretch into Tamanrasset and had to be towed in by a lorry. Unable to afford the camping fees they had parked on a bare wind-blown patch to spend Christmas and service their old ambulance. John looked red-eyed and pinched. He had been working night and day to get the van running again. Ann was a teacher and made a great hit with the boys feeding them dates and sweets. They were spirited and determined young people, battling against heavy odds, cold, hungry and short of money.

David came back to camp and took me out to meet them. "What's that gaping hole in the side of their van?" I asked as we approached the group. "That's where John has cut away a complete body panel to try and make an oven" replied David. "Just the man we need" called John, and as we arrived he was holding up the sheet of bent aluminium. "We haven't any bolts." While the men rummaged through our tool box I talked to the girls and suggested they should come to the camp and use our facilities and perhaps borrow our oven if their one was unsuccessful. We parted with promises of "see you tomorrow." "Let's have something special for supper" suggested Sarah, peering into the trailer. "All right" I said "how about trying out the oven, we'll have chicken and ham pies." We erected the camping stove and balanced it on the two petrol burners to warm up, using the water carriers as wind breaks. When the temperature on the dial read 250^0 I hopefully popped the tinned pies in and started preparing the rest of the food.

A loud bang followed by drumbeats and low clanking broke into the quiet evening. The Tuaregs were celebrating. "Oh! Let's go and see the dancing" clamoured the children with one voice "please!" "Get Daddy to take you and I'll keep an eye on the pies. Susan and I will go later." About an hour passed before they returned, Sarah imitating the dancing and Sean firing make believe muskets into the air. "You'll love it Mum" they said. "Where's supper?" I produced the pale, doughy half-cooked pies. Nothing would induce the temperature of the oven to rise over 250^0 as the ambient temperature dropped. We ate the gluey mess with liberal helpings of potato, everyone's appetite suddenly disappearing. "Do you think Santa will come" asked Peter winking at me. "You never know," I replied "you'd better hang up your stocking just in case. I expect he'll have to use a camel out here."

They romped off to bed and hung up grubby misshapen socks on the bamboo slats near their pillows. Five minutes later they were asleep and Susan and I slipped away in the Land Rover to see the celebrations. Following the noise of the drums and quick instructions from David, I wound through the dark streets into a narrow lane and parked near a small unlit square. "Don't leave me" said Susan nervously. "I'm not" I replied. "We'll leave the Land Rover lights on, but we'll lock it up." Walking slowly past the black houses and doorways there was a loud bang. Susan clawed at the back of my jacket. An uneasy silence seeped over the square. "Let's go back" said Susan, clutching my arm firmly and heading for the Land Rover "they're finished anyway."

I backed up and drove towards the camp gates as Susan lit a cigarette and drew deeply. We were almost back when I heard the drums start up again. "I want to see the dancing" I said, swinging the Land Rover round again. "You sit inside with the doors locked if you like." Walking down the dark lane once more, Susan unwilling to be left close behind, I approached the square. It was very eerie and a little frightening, the only light coming from two small hurricane lamps. With their drums beating rhythmically, the Arabs danced around and chanted, faces obscured by their hoods. I crept nearer to get a better view while Susan clung to the shadow of the houses. It seemed so unreal and so far removed from Christmas at home. Suddenly there was another loud bang as the men swung round and fired muskets into the air and then into the sand at our feet. I backed away feeling an intruder and this time we did go back to the camp and bed.

Christmas morning starts early for anyone with children. "Look what I've got" said an excited voice from the room next door. "So have I, look" said another. The sound of rustling paper, squeals of delight and cries of 'swop you' filtered through. Although we were still half asleep, at 6 a.m. three happy faces appeared with big hugs and kisses as everyone came in for a cuddle. "Don't move Mummy" said Sean "We've got a surprise for you" and three children disappeared back to their rooms. A guitar strummed, followed by a giggle. "Are you going to Scarborough fair? Parsley, sage, rosemary and thyme" sang the three young voices. I listened to one of my favourite tunes, brushing away a sentimental tear and smiling affectionately at David. After loud applause and lots more hugs and kisses, I asked them "But when did you learn it?" "Oh that was easy" they explained "Every time you disappeared for a few minutes to go to the loo or have a shower we dropped everything and practiced like mad." I laughed, poor David—no wonder he had made such slow progress with his work in the last few days.

Richard had promised he would dress up for Christmas and he called in to the children to come out and inspect him. He looked magnificent with his black curly hair and beard, and clad in a black velvet suit trimmed with white and high heeled boots. The children went off arm in arm with him to take the breakfast room by storm.

Later in the morning Ann and Rosemary, the two girls from the white ambulance, arrived with towels tucked under their jackets. They went off for a shower and shampoo and re-joined us with Richard and Miriam for Christmas lunch. Ann produced fresh dates, Miriam some anchovies and I made pancakes for two hours, which we ate with lashings of maple syrup followed by tinned fruit cake and cheese. I rescued a battered box of crackers out of the trailer for the children and we had a hilarious, if rather different, Christmas day in the warm sunshine.

It was over all too soon. We all drifted back to our chores and preparations. It was not without some apprehension that each group contemplated the next more hazardous section of the desert and we all tried to glean as much information as possible from people who had just completed it on their way north. Apparently there was an alternative route via Arlit, a French mining town with many facilities, and sounding very attractive, as the standard route involved a 500 mile stretch to Agadez without petrol or water depots. However, no-one had a route marked on a map, not even the desert police in Tamanrasset when David made a quick trip to their office for advice. Even if we got there, one group told us, the route south from Arlit was extremely difficult and little used. The odds sounded too high, so we settled for the standard route to Agadez.

As David poured over the map Peter tapped him gently on the shoulder "Daddy, I think you'd better come and look at Richard's engine" he said, "He doesn't seem to understand that points in the distributor should open." David wandered across and picking up an old razor blade showed Richard how to adjust the points by slipping it between them. When Richard started up the engine David was horrified to find that the only way to keep it going was for Richard to rotate the starting handle accompanied by showers of sparks around the hole in the front bumper, he had no earthing strap! After more technical explanations Richard headed out of the main gate, returning ten minutes later with a perfect earthing strap, given to him by a man with a Fiat. They bolted it on, the children piled in and they all headed north into the desert for a test run.

David returned smiling and shaking his head "They'll never get to South Africa, let alone Australia" he said "but at least they'll have a lot of laughs trying." Susan and I packed up most of our belongings and gear.

David had booked a table at the little hotel for supper and we planned an early get away next morning for the next stage of our journey. All dressed and ready for going out on the town in our best clothes, two English boys knocked at the door of the hut. They had just arrived in their Land Rover and had been casting admiring glances at our vehicle and equipment. Newly qualified mechanical engineers, they immediately embarked on long technical discussions with David about gearboxes and free wheeling hubs. They had spare gaskets, they announced when David told them of his improvisation and a 'knock' in the gear box. Susan and I smiled benignly and longed for supper. At last we got it, lamb chops, cabbage and a very welcome bottle of wine. The six of us walked back to the camp arm in arm singing Christmas carols and going over the day. Three tired, happy children were soon asleep and Susan cuddled in her sleeping bag with a book. "I don't feel like going to bed yet" I whispered to David. "Let's go for a drive" he said, holding out his hand and closing the Land Rover door quietly, we crept out of the camp and into the desert, parked in the middle of nowhere and counted the stars.

CHAPTER 5

LOST . . .

SUDDENLY RESTLESS AND eager to be on our way, everyone was up early on Boxing Day. After affectionate farewells to Richard and Miriam, who had teamed up with the English boys in the Land Rover for the next section, we waved goodbye to our friends on the camp site and drove down to the police station for clearance. John and Ann from the ambulance were already there, together with two other groups in Volkswagen vans.

"I'll stand in the queue with Sean and complete all the paper work, if you take the Land Rover to the petrol station and fill up the jerry cans" said David. "I filled up both the tanks yesterday." It was difficult to see the petrol pumps, there were cars everywhere and huge Trans-Saharan lorries boxed in the sides. "If I ever get to the front of the queue, I'll never get out again" I muttered to Susan, chewing my finger nails, "I'll have to back away and I can't with the trailer hitched on, it will jack-knife on me as soon as I try." I peered anxiously into the driving mirror as more cars closed up behind me. "Stop worrying Mummy, I'll tell you what to do" reassured Peter. I continued to glance nervously from one side to another as cars parked closer and closer. I simply could not hit anything at this stage and damage our equipment. "Pull it forward . . . round a bit . . . nearer!" shouted an Arab in desperation as I crept up to the pumps, the nose of the Land Rover almost touching a large lorry. Peter unlocked the jerry cans and supervised their filling while I stood around wringing my hands. Short of growing wings I could not see where to go next. Horns started blowing as the customer behind grew impatient and I scowled at them hoping to frighten them away. Counting my change carefully, I climbed back into the driving seat and started up the engine. There was only about two feet between the trailer and the haphazardly parked cars behind me. The drivers were out of their seats, hands on hips, no-one prepared to move an inch. I shunted forwards and backwards as the excited Arabs ran around me shouting and waving their arms. The trailer jack-knifed! "This" I said firmly, "is just ridiculous." "It's no good them standing there rolling their eyes to the heavens, they've got to give me more room." Forgetting all my French in my embarrassed agitation, I harangued the groaning Arabs in English. "Either that lot there have got to move" I said, pointing at the now even larger mass of cars behind me "or those two lorries in front have to." And I folded my arms and sat tight lipped in front of the wheel. The horns wailed monotonously and continually in my ears and I wiped my damp palms down the legs of my jeans. Susan sat with head down, her red flush rapidly catching up with mine and Sarah and Peter knew better than to break the tense silence inside the Land Rover.

Eventually the two lorry drivers emerged from the cigarette shop encouraged by the young Arab from the petrol pumps. They surveyed the scene and smiled at me not unsympathetically. Stubbing out their half smoked cigarettes they climbed into their cabs. After much revving and belching of fumes, the two lorries backed out on to the road leaving me a clear path. "Go on, go on!" yelled the Arabs, glad to see the back of me, and fell about laughing as I let the clutch in too quickly and we kangarooed out of the petrol station. "Well done Mummy" said Peter trying to soothe my injured pride, as I straightened up and parked on the side of the road.

"Be a darling Susie" I said "and go and see if they have any cigarettes in the shop, I can't face them." She reappeared three minutes later shaking her head. Oh well, we had got half a packet left and it was 1200 miles to Kano. We would just have to give it up. Poor David!

Re-joining Sean and David at the police station, we found they had had an equally frustrating time. The three other groups had not reported to the police when they had arrived at Tamanrasset and all their paper work was incomplete. The officials had given them a very hard time and been very uncooperative and long winded. Fortunately, when David at last got to the desk, Sean beamed at the policeman and shook him eagerly by the hand, making instant friends, our paper work was all in order and it only took a few minutes to complete the formalities.

Waiting for us outside, David popped his foot up against a long low fence to tie his shoelace and staggered forward into a heap as the whole fence collapsed—right in front of the Military Police Headquarters! He was immediately surrounded by angry soldiers who nudged and shooed him away as he tried to put right the damage and prop up the fence again. We suddenly felt we wanted to get away from all these people and back into the desert for a bit of peace and quiet.

There was only one more thing to do before heading for the customs post on the outskirts of town. We still had $30 worth of Algerian currency left, which we did not need and we were forbidden to take out of the country. We went to the bank to change it back to French francs. "It's quite simple" explained the bank clerk patiently, "there's no money in the bank, I can't change it." "But we'll be leaving Algeria in the desert and we're not allowed to take it out of the country" David pointed out. The clerk shrugged his shoulders—as if to say that is your problem and turned his attention to the next customer.

"Now what do we do?" I asked David as we stood looking at each other outside the bank. "Everybody in" called David, pointing at the Land Rover and obviously having made a decision. We drove back to the camp site and watched silently while he sat round a table with a group of the Germans from the 'rolling hotel' working out figures on a scrap of paper. Ten minutes later he stood up, shook hands all round. "Danke schoen, aufweidersehen" he called at the group as he climbed back into the driving seat and swung the Land Rover around and out of the gates once more.

There only remained the customs post then we would be away at last. The ambulance and two Volkswagens were already there as we drew up next to the flagpole. The children were all set to stand around chattering but were well schooled by this stage in coping with officialdom. They crowded into the little office, smiling angelically and shaking hands all round. We were cleared in record time and Peter rushed over to me to show me a sentence in Arabic which the customs officer had written in his diary for him.

As we pulled away the other engines sprang into life and the three vehicles followed us in convoy. They seemed anxious not to lose David. We felt our way gingerly at first on the corrugation, getting the feel of desert driving again. The grey slate soon gave way to sand in all directions and we tested it carefully before pulling off for two short stops to eat during the day. We soon lost sight of our followers and even when we decided to stop at 3 o'clock after only 68 miles for the day, they did not catch up or pass us. There was quite a wind getting up so we decided to erect the big tent. By working in three teams of one adult and a child to each section, had got our time down to a very satisfactory 10 minutes. It was a cosy night and everyone slept well.

The clear sky and brilliant sun of the very early morning quickly changed to heavy grey clouds and the wind whipped up the sand into swirling stinging needles as we screwed up our eyes and sheltered our faces with raised arms. We tied large scarves around our mouths and noses, put on sunglasses and firmly knotted our anorak hoods under our chins. The children braced themselves, leaning forward into the increasing wind as we stared ahead looking for the next marker or cairn. Drifting sand covered the distinguishing corrugation and visibility dropped steadily. We carefully logged anything of any significance, a strange pile of stones, a burnt out wreck, making detailed notes of time, mileage on the speedometer and compass direction.

Suddenly we saw in the distance a long line of dry trees, fuzzy round the edges and waving in the wind; but as we drew closer the outlines cleared and the trees became camels splayed legged and meandering aimlessly across the sand with two Tuaregs riding cowboy. "They look magnificent" said Susan groping in her bag. "I must get a photograph." But as she raised her camera the leading rider waved his arms and shook his head—no photographs! We waited as he rode up to the open window on his frothing camel and greeted him in French. He wanted water he indicated holding up an empty goat skin, and matches too. They all wanted matches. I felt sure we would run out of them ourselves at the rate we had been giving them away. Pleased with the box I gave him and his full goat skin he signalled to his friend to draw closer and together they posed, making the camels kneel and then stand up as we took all the pictures we wanted whilst behind them their unladen caravan strayed off in all directions. As we slowly drove away, we heard a shout and looked round to see one of the Tuaregs running after us waving the box of matches. "I wonder what his problem is" said David, as we stopped once more. "I know" I replied, as the Arab thrust the open box into my hand and pointed at the black ends of the matches. "He's used to red-tipped ones and these are safety matches." I took one out and struck it to show him that they worked and without a word he took back the box and walked away.

We struggled on in very disagreeable conditions keeping a wary eye on the compass and making very slow progress. Fooled by the drifting sand time after time, we clambered out as the vehicle shuddered to a halt in the soft conditions and unbolted the sand ladders. Panting and gasping as the wind and sand buffeted us, we all dug round the wheels with hands and shovels and the children pushed until they fell in a heap exhausted. It was no good even trying to light the cooker to make a warm meal, so we all crouched in the back of the Land Rover and made do with bread and marmite and cheese, followed by orange squash. Throughout the early afternoon, the weather deteriorated more and more and despite our careful navigation, the track became increasingly difficult to discern. "I've lost sight of the Piste" said Susan anxiously, as we climbed out yet again to start digging about 2 p.m. "Me too" I replied, trying to keep the alarm out of my voice as the children helped me to scoop out channels in front of the wheels and wedge in the sand ladders. All around us there was nothing but soft sand and grey jagged boulders craning like drowning men to keep their tips above the advancing ground. "I can fly" shouted Sarah as the wind crept inside her anorak and blew it up into a fat tense misshapen balloon and she flapped her arms up and down. "Come back and dig" I called "whilst Susan and I walk on and try to find the track."

Susan headed off in one direction, I picked my way through the boulders in the other, glancing over my shoulder every few minutes to make sure the others were still in sight. My scarf slipped down around my neck and a quick intake of breath filled my mouth with sand and set my cheeks tingling as I took the full force of the blast in my face. Spitting and grinding the gritty dust between my teeth I turned and looked back at our lonely distant Land Rover and the tiny figures of my children hunched on their knees digging furiously around the wheels. Far in the opposite direction I saw Susan scouting on but no reassuring wave. Head down, heavy feet, bending low against the wind, she trudged dejectedly back. Visibility was appalling. No pole or cairn to guide us, nothing but deep soft sand, knife edged boulders and darkness approaching. "No sense of responsibility, unnecessary danger, madness" screamed the critics in my ears. The three children paused for breath as I approached peering hopefully through sand covered sunglasses, faces masked by large scarves. I shook my head; they shrugged their shoulders and carried on digging. The Sahara, like the sea was showing us its many moods. Another thousand miles still lay ahead. The bleached white camel bones mocked me. "We seem to have lost the Piste" I told David quietly "but there is a big old wrecked van not far ahead, it may give us some shelter." We pushed and grunted as the wheels gripped the ladders and staggered forward and then we trudged wearily behind as David fought to keep our strange caravan moving through the unrelenting deep sand. He pulled up alongside the large old van, tipped on its side and half full of drifting sand. The wind moaned in and out of the blackened interior and a loose strip of metal sang high pitched songs of travellers long gone. Heaving and leaning against the naked frame we satisfied ourselves that it was firm and solid before quickly unfolding the awning and tying the guy ropes to it, jumping to catch the billowing canvas as it headed skywards. While the children collected large stones to weigh down our edges, Susan and I crouched inside and unpacked the cooker. "Shit" spat Susan, throwing another dead match into the sand. "Sugar" I reminded her, glancing up to see if the children were in earshot. "Oh all right, sugar but it doesn't relieve my feelings half as much" We got the kettle on and helped David to drag the sleeping bags off the roof rack, clutching wildly but unsuccessfully as a large polythene sheet took flight into the closing gloomy dusk.

Sean tore off after it throwing handfuls of sand into the air, tumbling and scrambling over the rocks and came back triumphantly, the wind wrapping it round him like a cocoon.

Huddled together in our small shelter, we squatted in the sand drinking welcome hot coffee and eating supper. We had plenty of water, a trailer full of food and reasonable shelter. We could afford to sit back and wait until the weather felt in a better mood.

As darkness fell and we were climbing into our sleeping bags, we heard the sound of car engines. Rushing out we saw three sets of headlights wavering and flashing in the distance as they approached us. It was a convoy of two Range Rovers and a Toyota Land Cruiser with an Italian and German crew—plus Arab guide we discovered—as they all piled out looking aghast at our party of young children and women. "Which way is the Piste?" asked the driver of the leading car. "We're not sure" shouted David above the wind. "We think it should be that way according to our compass"—he pointed into the night. "We've decided to wait until the morning and see if conditions improve." "Are you the only man in the group?" he asked slightly horrified—"what about water, have you got plenty, if you have to stay for a few days?" "We're fine thank you" David reassured him. "Well stocked with everything except cigarettes—you haven't any spare cigarettes we could buy have you? My wife and her friend are gasping." "You haven't any?" he said addressing me, he was obviously a smoker and could imagine the agony. "Well yes" I laughed, "we have got a couple left, but we're trying to save them." He returned from his car a few minutes later and pressed two packets into my hand. "Please let me pay you" I pleaded. "Nonsense" he replied "buy me a drink in Agadez when you get there. I think we will try and press on."

They all climbed back into their cars and started up the engines. The Land Cruiser took the lead and had no trouble getting underway but the Range Rover backed in its own tracks packing down the sand to make a firm 'runway' before slipping into forward gear. Even so they were soon in trouble wallowing and fighting to keep moving as their wheels sank deeper and deeper. We all rushed forward as their crews bailed out to lighten the load, and helped push the cars onto firmer ground. With shouts and waves of encouragement from the children they eventually pulled away and we watched as the red lights winked erratically, quickly disappearing from sight leaving us with the empty darkness and unrelenting wind. "Right everyone to bed" I suggested, "we want to make an early start in the morning if it looks half reasonable." "No-one even thought about washing. We just peeled off our anoraks and climbed into sandy sleeping bags, lying like a row of sausages on the plastic cover. David switched off the torch and worked his way down trying to edge out the sharp stone under my back. A relaxed sigh froze on my lips, I lay perfectly still. Something small had just wriggled across my legs. Lying in the darkness, I tentatively moved one foot. Nothing happened, then the other one. I could hear the steady breathing from the rest as sleep sought each of them out and soothed their tired bodies. Fumbling and groping above my head, my hand closed round the torch when a scream shattered the stillness. "Something just crawled all over my face and ran down Sarah's sleeping bag" shouted Peter—clambering up as I snapped on the light. "Keep still, keep still" I urged as I flashed the torch in all directions. "Something moved, under the Land Rover, there Mummy." I swung round the torch and paused, two little red eyes, and twitching nose stared back at us and then scampered behind the wheel. "It's only a mouse." laughed David" It won't hurt you. Come on, everyone, back to sleep." We cuddled down again as our little visitor returned making frantic attempts to get on top of the food box at my feet. I fell asleep to the monotonous rhythm of the little creature jumping and falling back onto my legs with a plop as it tried in vain to reach the scattered crumbs on the lid.

"There's someone about out there" whispered David in my ear. "I'm going to have a look." I peered at my watch. It was midnight. Dragging back the side of the awning, I could hear muffled shouts and see dim lights over to the right. It was an Arab lorry, stuck. Vague shapes moved about and bent round the wheels. "Oh no" I groaned "I hope they don't see us and want us to help dig out, I couldn't stand it." We watched silently for half an hour until at last the truck crept forward and the Arabs jumped aboard. "Thank goodness for that" muttered David as he checked round our camp and crawled back over me to his bed. "The wind seems to have dropped a bit. Did you hear the rain at 9 o'clock?" I whispered. "Rain", you're joking" he said. "No, truly there was a heavy shower of rain. The wind disappeared quite a bit afterwards. It'll probably be a lot better by the morning." We cuddled close and went back to sleep.

"Come on, get up you lazy lot" said Susan grabbing the pillows from under our sleepy heads. "Go away" I muttered "it's still dark." "It's almost 6 o'clock, you must get up. It's the early bird that gets the worm" she replied, trotting out one of her many platitudes, always guaranteed to stir a response from me. "I don't like worms" I growled—kicking off my blanket. "I wish you wouldn't be so jolly in the morning, at least not until we've had a cup of coffee." How she put up with my constant reluctance to get up in the morning I'll never know, perhaps in the same way that I put up with the virtuous faces of her and David standing over me, except I was never as nice about it.

The wind had dropped a lot, although it still blew quite strongly and we zipped on anoraks to keep out the cold air. The ground felt much firmer in the early morning and there was very little sand lifting in the gusts. Visibility was much better. Straining and screwing up our eyes we saw a tiny blob on the horizon which looked like a marker and decided to head for it. It was slow going with frequent shouts from David of "everybody out" as our speed dropped and we flung open the doors and leapt out of the still moving Land Rover. I usually fell flat on my face, never quite getting up enough forward momentum as I landed. On one near disastrous occasion, Susan never athletic at the best of times, slipped and almost went under the back wheel. We decided she was not up to this sort of gymnastics yet and must stay put in future, leaving the heroics to the children and myself.

We all needed a hot meal, but it was quite obvious we would never be able to light the stove in such a high wind and anyway it was too cold to stand around for more than a few minutes. The heavy grey clouds and empty horizon made it hard to forget our rumbling stomachs, but then we saw our 'soup kitchen'. The route across the Sahara was littered with the burnt-out shells of vehicles that never made it. And there lay an old Volkswagen van, on it's side and half filled with sand. We checked that it was stable and set the children on scooping out the sand whilst Susan and I slid off the trailer lid and selected some tins and packets. There was not a lot of room and we had to squat inside with our backs against what had once been the roof but at least it was sheltered from the wind and the cooker lit without any trouble. The children climbed into the driving compartment and made up a great game filtering sand through the holes and light sockets. It really was too ridiculous for words, we felt, as we patiently waited for the kettle to boil, huddled in the tiny space, and as David got out his camera to take a photograph. "Think of the marvellous captions you could put to his picture" laughed Susan "Family runs out of funds living in dire circumstances in Algeria", or what about "N.H.S. doesn't pay its doctors enough." "Smile" said David and clicked the camera as we turned to look up through the gaping hole above our heads.

"Lunch up" I called, handing steaming plates through into the drivers cab to the children. "But Mummy it's raining" wailed Sarah. It was too, and a big drip landed on to the end of my nose and then another. "Everyone into the Land Rover then, and take your lunch with you." The shower was short lived and they were soon back trying to tear the exhaust system off the Volkswagen, while Susan and I washed up with one cereal bowl full of water, carefully tipping it into the next and sloshing it round with our fingers. "If that big Smash tin is empty, I know just what to use it for" David said, poking his head into our 'kitchen'. As I handed it out I caught the twinkle in his eye. "He's up to something" I said to Susan, and climbed over her and followed him to the trailer. He reached in and lifted out the gallon container of chutney, split and oozing, and plastered in sand.

"Oh no, I simply couldn't bear it!" I exclaimed, but David insisted on decanting the remains into the big tin and sticking down the lid with tape. "The next time it so much as drips, I'm putting it out" I insisted and went back to the Volkswagen with my tale of woe.

Before we left again, David wanted to inspect our second big fuel tank. As the main tank ran dry during the morning, we had switched over to the second one but no petrol had come through. He decided it must be a dirty filter and we topped up from our jerry cans, anxious to keep going.

As we packed away all our bits and pieces, he gave us the sad news. "It wasn't the filter" he said screwing on the filter cap "the tank is empty!" "But how can it be empty, you filled it yourself" cried Susan. "I know, but the jubilee clip is loose underneath and there's a slight staining on the chassis suggesting it may have drained out." he replied. "It must have happened on Christmas night when we left the Land Rover parked in the middle of the compound instead of near the hut in Tamanrasset." "How much have we got left?" I asked. "Not enough, four full jerry cans and what's left in the tank is not even enough to go back." "Well in that case, we'll have to go on and work it out when we run dry" I said hustling the children back to the Land Rover. In the early afternoon we arrived at In Guezzam at the Algerian border. A few scattered tents and a couple of camels squashed any hopes of getting fuel. We met up with another Land Rover carrying four Dutchmen, far from friendly, and totally disinterested in our problem when we asked if they had any extra petrol.

The border guard collected up our passports and disappeared behind a sand dune on the right only to reappear some 15-20 minutes later with them all stamped. We explained to him about our lack of fuel but he reassured us smilingly that they had a fleet of petrol driven Land Rovers at the Niger border. It sounded unlikely, but hopeful. Between In Guezzam and the Niger border there lay 16 miles of no-mans land with badly marked track and repeated long sections of deep soft sand. We all walked a large part of the way giving the occasional push as David struggled to keep the lightened vehicle moving. We could not imagine how some of the vehicles we had seen in Tamanrasset would ever get through that dreadful stretch. David let all our tyres down and had the Land Rover in 4 wheel drive, low ratio box all the way, but we still had to resort to sand ladders more than once. Towards the end the ground improved a little and David zigzagged and tacked up the slope, sometimes doing a complete figure-of-eight to gather more momentum on the down run before going on again. We had been doing a careful fuel consumption check over the previous few hours and were horrified to find we were only getting 7 miles to the gallon. We would not have had enough petrol even with our second tank at that rate. We talked again about Arlit the French mining town but felt hopelessly lost without a route map or any indication of the direction.

At Assamaka, the Niger border post, we could see irregular shapes on the horizon. We had to stop to top up the tank from a jerry can and the wheels spun again as we tried to pull away. Same old routine, out we got and pushed and grunted, trudging slowly behind as the Land Rover snaked up the slope. It looked like being a very long walk. David did not pause at all, but kept heading for the border. Tired and very dirty, the three children, Susan and myself linked arms and advanced slowly singing a marching song and refused to be down-hearted; and then we stopped with a hearty cheer as the Land Rover re-appeared without the trailer, coming back to pick us up.

The great metropolis of Assamaka with its petrol driven Land Rovers was unbelievable! It consisted of nothing but two small windowless mud huts and a bleak wind-swept stretch of barbed wire fence. Two large black vultures strutted impatiently round a warm rust-coloured spring that gushed out of the ground. There was no one in sight except the Dutchmen and their Land Rover. They seemed inclined to be a little friendlier this time, as two of them followed David and the boys over to the little hut and disappeared inside. Peter ran across to us a few minutes later and banged on my window. "Daddy wants two biros" he said and I rummaged in my bag. "Any problems" I asked. "I don't think so" he called as he ran off. Another ten minutes passed before they all re-appeared accompanied by two very official-looking soldiers. "This gentleman is a Colonel" said David, as he introduced us in French. "He wants to inspect our vehicle and luggage." "That could take a while" I muttered, climbing out and putting my bag into the Colonel's outstretched hand. He was a very thorough but very polite young man. He went through the inside of the vehicle, the outside and the roof rack then pointed to the trailer. "Oh well, I suppose we've been lucky so far" said Susan in a low voice as we untied the straps. The Colonel inspected the children's' toys, and tumbled the clothes around in each of the sail bags in turn. David's black shaving kit looked important so he unzipped it and felt around indiscriminately only to draw out his hand quickly with a gasp. Blood gushed down the back of his hand and soaked into the cuff of his jacket. He had sliced his finger on the razor! "Suck it" I said in English, pushing his hand up to his mouth and grabbing a box of tissues out of the trailer. He had suddenly lost interest in the rest of the luggage and signalled to us to pack it all up, while I wound up his finger. Maybe he'd learnt not to be quite so officious!

The only problem that remained was that vehicles were not allowed to cross the next section alone; they had to go in convoy. The Dutch team were anxious to be on their way but accepted with bad grace that they had to join up with us, although they admitted they were carrying a lot of extra fuel and would be able to help us out. When the police were satisfied that all the paper work was in order, the Dutch Land Rover drove off without so much as a wave, much too quickly for our heavily laden vehicle to catch up. We trundled off in our own time and started on the most badly marked section of Piste we had so far encountered. It quickly became a sort of game, who could spot the next pole as we drove over the flat featureless empty desert but, of course, many of the poles had been knocked flat and we relied more and more on our compass and a carefully written log.

At 2 o'clock, we decided to try and select a camp site. There really was not much choice. We rumbled on for an hour but there was nothing, no form of protection from the constant cold wind, no tree, no hill, no pile of stones. In the end we pulled up near a stack of slates about a foot high at least they would be useful to weigh down the sides of the awning. We did not bother about beds, again choosing to sleep on the ground and make the best of it. David got out our last bottle of whisky and carefully worked out our ration, running a piece of sticky tape down the side. We could each have one twenty seventh of a bottle per night he estimated, if it was to last us to Agadez. It was a terrible personal toss up whether to have a nip before or after supper!

Susan and I felt a bit choked; we had not had a decent wash for days. I had a quick chat with David and he suggested to the children that they went for a walk in the dark to study the night sky. Meanwhile Susan and I revelled in half a bucket of warm water and a change of clothes. They were all pretty disgusted with me when they got back and found a bowl of hot water waiting and a firm request to strip off and wash. "We don't mind being dirty Mummy" said Peter. "That's as maybe," I replied, "clothes off everyone—scrub."

It wasn't a good night. The cold wind sneaked underneath the Land Rover and blew across our faces making us restless and uneasy. Susan got up at 5 a.m. and climbed into the Land Rover to get warm, but there did not seem any point in rushing anywhere, we were very low on petrol now and had no clear idea what we were going to do about it. We made a leisurely start to the day, after investigating what at a distance looked like a large collection of eggs. They turned out to be gourds—the earth was not completely barren after all.

Well away from the Piste on the right a few palm trees and grazing camels came into view. We drew over and stopped to pump up our soft tyres and peel off our pyjamas as the sun was quite hot and we were beginning to perspire. No sooner had the Land Rover rolled to a halt than a little group of visitors came running across the sand from a tiny hut hidden among the palms. The first to arrive was a little girl of about 6 carrying her naked baby sister, quickly followed by their mother and a fine featured woman with skin stained a deep indigo. She gravely shook hands with us all and then squatted down to watch our every movement. I found a tube of sweets in the side pocket of my door and shared them between the children. As their little hands grasped each one and crammed them into their mouths, "Sucre, sucre" said the mother, stretching out a thin sun wrinkled hand. "De l'eau" as she pointed to the empty polythene container. These were the only two French words she seemed to know. Sugar was easy, I filled up an empty tin and gave it to her but I was reluctant to part with any water. I did not know where our next supply was coming from, or when. Sitting next to her on the ground I tried to explain our situation, she must have a source of water I was sure. Drawing pictures in the sand and making exaggerated hand movements I established there was a well at the next oasis Abangarit. "How far to Agangarit?" I got across to her. She pointed at the sun and made a complete circle with her arm and then pointed at one of the grazing camels. Abangarit was one day's journey by camel; that could not be very far by Land Rover.

Sean found one of his Dinky Toys and handed it to the eldest child. A wail of protest came from the little one and with a puckered disgruntled face she clawed and snatched at her sister. Children were the same the world over. We laughed and said goodbye to them all as the mother tapped my boots—she wanted shoes, she indicated, pointing at her bare hardened feet. We only had the ones we wore plus a pair of light weight sandals. I was sorry I could not help. They would have made a marvellous trade for her. They turned and walked slowly back to the cluster of trees as we drew away. The sun was beating down and we all peeled off another layer.

10 km later the somewhat bored and exasperated Dutch group were waiting for us and promised to see that we made it to Abangarit. We were down to just four gallons of petrol. However as before they took off at a spanking pace and we never saw them again. The firm Piste gave way to a long section of soft sand and our precious petrol level got lower and lower and swinging from one side to the other added miles to the basic distance. All out and shoulders braced

against the trailer, we were taken completely by surprise when a Land Rover, similar to our own but without trailer, drew alongside and three smiling cheerful Italians called out to us. They seemed to have appeared from nowhere. David stopped and went over to explain our predicament and they volunteered to ride tandem with us to Abangarit. A welcome party had rushed out to meet us as we approached, a large crowd of poverty stricken children covered with skin and scalp lesions and grossly infected eyes. They clawed at the sides of the vehicle and hung on dangerously as we slowed to avoid a group of very little ones sitting on the track. Low dark Arab tents were pitched under the few palms, draped with old rags and branches to keep out the cold night winds. "I'm going to have to leave you here darling and try and hitch a lift with this other Land Rover" David told me quietly. I looked round at all the little faces and heads bobbing up and down at the windows, hands trying to prise them open. "Not here" I said, horrified, "I'll never be able to protect all our gear. Try and take us on a little bit further, away from the tents." "All right, but I want to leave you enough petrol for cooking and it must be in walking distance if you need more water."

We picked up speed on the firm ground and drove for about a mile before David swung the Land Rover round and parked in the lea of a low sand dune, nearly out of sight of the track to the oasis. A quick chat with the Italians and our plans were laid. They would take David with them to Agadez 200 miles south and the main point of contact at the southern end of the desert. I quickly packed a bag with food, warm clothes and sleeping bag and in no time at all they were gone.

We stood in a forlorn group watching the trail of dust until it was out of sight before silently turning back to inspect our new home. "This is super" yelled Sean, "we can play in the sand all day long" and he tumbled and rolled down the side of the dune. I felt empty and heavy and more than a little apprehensive. "There's no playing until we've built a proper camp" I snapped, "We'll start with the tent." Susan climbed onto the roof and peeled back the cover. "Come on kids, catch these bits as I pass them down" she called impatiently. She was tense and worried and irritated by the children's lack of appreciation of our situation. "Oh no" groaned Peter "Here's our first visitor already." Perched on a skinny, frothing, fly-blown camel came a young lad of about 15. He came right up to us and sat staring with a grave serious face as the five of us struggled with the complexities of the tent, and very funny we must have looked. I tried speaking to him in French. He had his unhappy looking camel just on the spot we had elected to erect the tent. He did not understand. "We'll just have to carry on and hope he gets the message" I grunted, batting off the flies which buzzed from the camel onto us and back again. We swung the frame upright and I made a pleading gesture for him to move, but he sat there impassive while his wretched animal drooled and slavered and looked down its snooty nose. Feeling quite exasperated with our visitor, I dragged unsuccessfully at the canvas, wishing to heaven David would come back and bolster my shrinking confidence. There was a quick movement behind me. I swung round and watched while he jumped lightly to the ground, took a hold of the edge of the tent and spread it neatly over the frame, smoothing the sides and kicking away the odd stone. He stood back to admire his handiwork and held out his hand with a twinkle in his dark eyes; then without further ado mounted his camel and rode silently off towards the oasis. It took at least a couple of hours to get our camp sorted out and all the beds organised but at last we thankfully threw ourselves into a chair as the sun continued to beat down from a cloudless sky.

"I need another drink" gasped a red-faced Sarah clambering into the back of the Land Rover and pumping furiously at the water filter. I climbed up on to the bonnet to check our water reserve on the roof rack. We had two nearly full 5 gallon containers and one already in use and half empty. It should be enough but if the heat continued we would have to watch our intake and I did not know how long we would have to wait for David to come back. "We'll all have a good wash tonight" I announced, to accompanied groans from the children "And then all the water must be kept for drinking. We will have to clean ourselves with cream and cologne tissues." Their expressions changed to delight. "There's one other thing we must all be very fussy about if we have to live here for a few days. The far side of the sand dune over there we will call Lavender Hill. When you go to the 'loo' take a shovel with you and dig a deep hole."

The sun started to dip towards the horizon. We cooked and ate supper quickly before darkness fell, while Peter—now appointed as technical advisor—checked the Land Rover and fixed up the burglar alarms. As an afterthought I took a heavy walking stick from under the back seats and placed it at the side of my bed next to the tent door and zipped us all in for the night. Everyone slept surprisingly well. I woke as usual about every hour listening and glancing around the tent. Twice I quietly opened the zip of the door flap and peered out at the dark shape of the Land Rover. Nothing moved; all was well.

Well used to waking early, we stretched and yawned and inspected the day about 6 a.m. There was no need to leap up and dash about, we were not going anywhere and feeling lazy and relaxed we turned over for another half hour while Peter put the kettle on for coffee.

The sound of a car engine jerked us out of our indolence and we leapt out of bed dragging on jeans and trying to flatten our untidy hair. It turned out to be three Italian trucks travelling north. They parked alongside and all clambered out, chattering excitedly in broken English and French. The Land Rover and all its special equipment fascinated them. I proudly demonstrated all our extra dials and gauges and, of course, the 'cruise control'—something we had all found a tremendous advantage. A quick flick of the switch and the vehicle automatically maintained its speed giving a much needed rest to the throttle foot of the driver, and one of the group produced a camera and photographed it from every angle before getting down to mundane matters like our water reserve. I assured them we were perfectly all right but shamelessly scrounged cigarettes once more, offering them tinned food in exchange before they went on their way. It was only 7.30 a.m. It looked like being a long day.

Making the most of the warm sun, we hung out all the sleeping bags and blankets to air and rubbed sun cream on our noses that were getting sunburnt. The children played happily in the sand, Susan settled with a book and I found time to do some much needed mending of the trailer cover.

Visitors arrived in the middle of the morning—two Arabs on foot. They moved right into our camp and stared unblinkingly at us at very close quarters, speaking no French but shaking hands repeatedly with us all. One was either the village idiot or bursting to spend a penny, we decided, as he wound one leg round the other and bent over at right angles leering into Sarah's face, she sitting with a fixed uncertain smile. They wanted matches, biros and anything else we were willing to part with. We sat for an uneasy half hour nodding and smiling as they edged to the tent door curiously inspecting all our belongings. It looked as if they intended to go in and I scrambled to my feet and blocked their way. Holding out my hand I bade them a very firm "au revoir" and stood my ground. Giggling, they shuffled off round the edge of the sand dune. I climbed to the top to make sure they were on their way, watching while they stopped to inspect the bits and pieces we had given them. They were harmless enough, just very persistent and somewhat embarrassing company after the first ten minutes. The next pair turned up about an hour later and we repeated the whole scenario, wondering how long it would be before news of our presence filtered back to the oasis and the whole tribe came to have a look at us.

Looking south into the gathering heat-haze, strange black jagged shapes appeared on the horizon. Were they trees or people or perhaps the big one was a lorry. We watched for hours, but nothing came our way, none of those mysterious blobs came any closer. We played games, sought the shade of the tent and I made silent tentative plans about what I would do if David did not return in another three days, that was when I reckoned we would need more water and when I would assume he had run into major problems preventing his return. "Let us have pancakes for supper" pleaded the children. I had a large pack of instant batter mix. Why not? It took an age cooking one at a time and everyone wanting more and more but we had nothing better to do.

As on the previous night I battened down before dark after probing some suspicious looking holes near the tent. "I wonder what made them or lives in them" I said to Susan apprehensively. By the light of a small neon tube run off our spare battery, Susan read aloud to us as we snuggled down into fresh smelling sleeping bags, the children safely zipped inside the bedroom units of the tent. She was reading Prester John to them, a favourite from her childhood. *"The native drumbeats were heard over the Rooirand, the Whites waited in their homesteads in the gathering unease at the native uprisings"* she read, then snapped the book shut. "That's enough of that" she laughed nervously "with our leader off God knows where and you with only a walking stick to fend off the local tribesmen."

We slept soundly. The stars twinkled at me when I stuck my head out in the early morning for a quick inspection and a friendly little mouse scurried past. No-one rolled out until 8 a.m. to scan the horizon. It was empty, absolutely empty. Nothing moved, the still warm Saharan silence settled on to us like a heavy blanket.

The children as usual were in great spirits eating breakfast hungrily and settling down to a game of schools, of all things. Young voices made us all pause in our activities and Sean scrambled up to the top of the sand dune. A group of children three boys and a darling little girl of about 9 were chasing a runaway donkey that had strayed from the nearby oasis. They drew back when they saw him, shy and a little afraid but as we waited four pairs of eyes appeared over the top of the sand, then led by the little girl they ventured closer and finally came into our camp. They were bright, lively little buttons, speaking a little French and very curious to find out why we were camping there. Was it water, or tyres or petrol we needed they wanted to know? Not wanting any details of our predicament to go back to the oasis, I reassured them that we were just tired and needed a rest. I dug out some French comics for the boys and biros for the girls and suddenly mindful of their lost donkey, they politely shook hands and disappeared.

About noon we saw two shimmering black silhouettes coming towards us from the oasis, but just then vehicles approached us from the south and they stopped, hovering like crows on the periphery. It was a convoy of three French cars, we discovered when they stopped. "Is that you" asked the leading driver pointing to his jerry can. Scrawled in David's familiar hand was "McMullan, Abangarit." I whooped with joy.

"When did you see him? Where did you see him?" I demanded in very ungrammatically correct French. They had seen him in Agadez, they told me. I heaved a thankful sigh of relief; at least he had got there. "Was he all right, when is he coming back?" I hopped around in the sand like a child. "Perhaps today, probably tomorrow" they assured me. I felt light headed, elated, ready for anything. "They've seen Daddy!" I shouted to the children "When is he coming back?" they clamoured. "Tomorrow probably" I answered, not wanting to raise their hopes too high. Their faces fell a little. "Perhaps it will be today" said Peter hopefully. "It's a long way darling, but he won't be too long now" I reassured him as we thanked the French group for their welcome news and waved until they were out of sight.

As the cars disappeared to the north, the two dark forms re-started their slow journey towards us. It was the little girl of earlier with her girl friend. They were delightful children and soon settled in with our three who produced balloons and paper aeroplanes and then played 'hide and seek'. A local Arab lorry hammered across the desert close by and the two little girls disappeared quickly behind the tent, whispering and laughing and peeping cautiously around the corner, only to reappear clapping their hands triumphantly when they were undiscovered.

It was a long, long afternoon. Twilight approached and the numerous hazy shapes on the skyline disappeared with the setting sun, leaving it empty and straight. We prepared for another early, lonely night when a local truck appeared in the far distance making a quick path over the desert between the grazing camels. Then suddenly it veered towards to us and headed straight for our camp. We stood in a silent group as it drew closer and closer and the boys moved forward, only to stop, shout, leap into the air with a cry of joy and swing each other round as they yelled "It's Daddy, it's Daddy, look, look, right up on top, there's Daddy!" Sure enough perched 12 feet up on sacks of groundnuts surrounded by about 20 Africans was David, looking tired and worn but grinning broadly. I did not know whether to laugh or cry as he clambered down. I flung my arm round his neck, the children launched themselves on him from behind and we gave him a hero's welcome, watched by his amused fellow travellers. He had brought the petrol we so badly needed, 30 gallons in large polythene jerry cans which he had bought off the Italians who had taken him to Agadez—and that was not all, he produced four cartons of cigarettes and a bottle of whisky to celebrate! We were all so excited and so very pleased to see him back. All thoughts of an early night disappeared as we led him over to a chair. It was New Year's Eve and we really had something to celebrate.

He had eaten practically no warm food for three days and had very little sleep. I put on a large pan of curry and while it bubbled away we drank a toast to his safe return. He had quite a tale to tell but tucked the children into their beds with little snippets to whet their appetites and promised a full account next day. "I think I'll sleep outside tonight" he announced, taking a deep breath of the crisp cool air and gazing up at the beautiful starlit sky. "Rather you than me" laughed Susan as I dragged my bed out to join him. When the others slept, we silently climbed up the side of the sand dune and began our recount of the stars, so happy to be together again.

CHAPTER 6

SAHARA SUCCESS . . .

"I'VE GOT NEWS for you all" David held out his watch for us to inspect. "Niger time is different, it's only 5 o'clock not 6." "Let's go back to bed" pleaded Sarah thrusting herself into the Land Rover out of the cold morning air. "Not on your life" said David chaffing her cold hands "if we leave now, we should get to Agadez tonight. Let's see how quickly we can get away." We packed in record time and looked back affectionately at the little niche in the sand dunes that had given us shelter for 4 days as we rumbled off.

The sun soon warmed us and we discarded anoraks and pullovers, littering the seats as we drove through fascinating and ever-changing scenery. The land changed from blank desert and sand to one of savannah, still very flat but with slowly increasing signs of dying vegetation. The jade green of huge melon-like gourds blended with the stunted thorn trees and bushes with wickedly sharp two inch thorns and tiny mimosa-like blooms. Rippling miles of wispy flaxen-coloured dead grass reminded us of autumn cornfields at home and masked the brown dry dusty soil, a clinging powder which filtered through every crevice and crack in the Land Rover.

This was part of the Sahel, a sad dying land choked and killed by continuous drought and being malignantly swallowed by the advancing desert. Along one long stretch of bare earth we saw pile after pile of camel bones as if a whole caravan had fallen where it stood. Hovering in the distance were ugly black broad-winged vultures, and small white ones like large sea gulls.

Near centres of population around artesian wells there were still some signs of life. Small fluttery birds like finches skittered alongside and in front of the vehicle, and occasional plump ones flying like game birds, rose into the air. Herds of goats grazed lazily and huge black oxen with very white, long, straight horns lumbered around. At all these little villages the children came rushing out, always hopeful that the truck would stop and leave something behind.

We sought the shade of a few trees for lunch close to the Piste, stepping out onto the brown earth which looked so firm but which rose in thick clouds of dust and lapped over the top of our boots. In no time we had two visitors weaving their way through the thorn bushes driving a goat and a donkey with its foal. We bought a couple of refreshing, although bitter tasting water melons from them but resisted their persistent attempts to sell us their goat. Strangely unfriendly compared with previous Arabs we had met; they peered into the Land Rover and demanded cigarettes, then David's sheath knife and finally wandered off without another word.

We made it a short break; we had Agadez in our sights and listened in admiring silence while David recounted his adventures of the previous few days as we ate up the miles. When he had left us at Abangarit he and the Italians had driven nonstop and late into the night to reach Agadez and the camp site. Exhausted and hungry he had curled up in his sleeping bag on the rough ground near the tents, spending a few cold uncomfortable hours thinking out his plans for getting back to us. Next morning he bought 5 large polythene jerry cans from the Italians, they no longer needed them now that the worst stretch of the desert travel was over and he produced a tin of sausages for breakfast much to their delight. These kind and generous people, two men and a woman, gave him hot drinks and took him into town to try and organise a lift back to Abangarit on a local lorry and report our non-arrival to the police. As luck would have it one of the lorry drivers standing around in the market place had heard on the desert grapevine about our Land Rover and a group of women and children stranded near the oasis. How that message filtered through we will never know. The driver agreed to give David a lift and showed him a dusty narrow little street in the town. "Be here at 3 this afternoon" translated Mahmoud, a bright young lad well dressed in European type clothes, who had appointed himself as David's helper and guide.

Anxious not to miss the lorry's departure, David hauled the full jerry cans round to the little street a few minutes before the appointed time only to be horrified when he saw "his lorry" jacked up and its back axle in pieces on the ground. There was nothing else for it. He squatted Arab fashion on his luggage and waited, it looked like being a long job. Mahmoud soon sought him out and was quickly joined by another little friend who stood guard over David's belongings while guided by Mahmoud, he shopped for cigarettes and whisky.

Huddled in the gutter once more, he shivered as the lengthening shadows shut out the last rays of the sun. Nearby an Arab skewered pieces of dried camel meat on sticks and cooked them in a small open fire and David's stomach contracted as the smell wafted over. He bought some and chewed slowly for a long time on the tough, dry meat, washing it down with crude red wine from a large flagon.

It was 9 o'clock before the lorry was repaired and loaded, stacked 12 feet high with sacks of groundnuts and no obvious space left for passengers. Two Frenchmen joined him, also planning to travel on the lorry and they watched heads tilted back as the Arabs tightened strong metal hawsers round their load to prevent it breaking loose on the unmerciful corrugation.

"All aboard" indicated the driver at last, and the three of them clambered up with David tying himself on to one of the hawsers and stacking his luggage as best he could. With a roar, the lorry started up and swept round the corner and stopped. To his utter disbelief a further group of 20 Arabs and Africans from many parts, each with their own luggage, swarmed up the bulging sacks and arranged themselves on top. They were all coming too! Then began the most uncomfortable journey of David's life. Hour after hour they swayed and bumped across the desert track in the bitterly cold night air. Twice they broke down and all the passengers, huddled in groups, sat watching, silently, while the lorry driver and his mate jacked up the lorry and made the necessary repairs. There was a further stop when the co-driver built a small fire and cooked a sort of couscous. David opened a tin of cheese and watched hungrily as the meat smoked and darkened in the flames. He passed his flagon of wine to the Frenchmen. They had made no provision for food or drink on the trip and their limbs were stiff with cold.

David's constant source of anxiety throughout the night was that he would not find us in the desert. The driver spoke no French so communication was impossible and because of the stops and repairs he could not work out any vague average speed and thus estimate the mileage covered. But all was well; the Arab knew just where we were in that vast wilderness. When they eventually arrived at our camp, I shook him by the hand, I was deeply grateful.

We had a hard day's drive, all very hot, very dirty and smelly and arrived in Agadez about 4 p.m. It was a fairly large, bustling town with dirt roads and a straggly collection of mud houses, converging on a large central market place. A strangely shaped water tower caught our attention as David guided and directed us with the confidence of a local inhabitant. We went straight to the hotel, the one and only, run by a well-dressed, prosperous looking Frenchman. All day David had spurred us on with tales of ice cold beer and showers, we could not wait.

The Land Rover was surrounded by children and youths on all sides as we drew up at the front door. One tapped on the window and grinned at David. It was Mahmoud. He had been awaiting our arrival and he immediately assumed the position of guardian to our vehicle, shouting and pushing all the other children away.

"First lead me to the beer" gasped Susan as we all staggered out and locked the doors. Chilled lager appeared on the counter as we entered the dimly lit, cool bar and we drank thirstily and silently for a few minutes before stretching back in our chairs with a satisfied, contented smile. The children did not sit still for long. They downed their orange and rushed outside to keep a watchful eye on all our belongings and chat to the curious bystanders. Sean as usual, friend of the world, soon came back clasping the hand of one young man and announced that this was his friend and he wanted to buy him a drink and could he please have some money for the disabled man outside the door. If we could gather together all the friends Sean made on our African trip, they would fill a large hotel. A gregarious and outgoing child, he approached everyone with confidence and a ready smile. Adults and children alike attached themselves to him everywhere we stopped and finding him for meals and bedtime was a constant problem.

David had investigated the hotel during his unhappy first visit to the town. It boasted a hot shower with the best room but the price was the equivalent of $7.50 a night. We could not all afford to stay there so we decided to split the arrangements. Susan and Sarah were to enjoy the luxury the first night while the rest of us camped, and David and I would move into the hotel for the second night. The boys did not think much of our plan—they ended up camping both nights and felt it was very unfair.

Susan and I unpacked all our toilet bags and clean clothes and together with Sarah headed straight for the shower while David took the boys off to find the camp site and put up the tent. The bedroom was cold, bare and windowless, it's only furnishing being two very old beds and a threadbare square of carpet on the stone floor. As I drew aside a long curtain over the doorway to the shower room, the brass rail cracked round my head and the curtain rings jangled onto the floor. The bathroom was equally bare. A small basin and cracked mirror were fixed on one wall and a slight depression in the concrete floor with thick pale sludge round the outlet hole comprised the shower. The main attraction however hung proudly in the corner, a large immersion heater. We turned on the tap but the water was icy cold. Following the wires and cables which snaked precariously across the walls, I flicked switches and turned all the knobs and waited. The water remained cold. We tried to trace the wiring circuit all over again but it was no good. Admitting defeat, Susan sought the Patron, who inspected the installation quickly assuring us that it had been working just the previous day in fact, but now it appeared to be broken. He would bring a man to repair it next day. Oh well a cold shower was better than no shower and much more stimulating we reassured each other as we dropped our filthy clothes in a pile and gasped as the water streamed through our hair. Shampooed, scrubbed and glowing we filed back to the bar to wait for David and made enquiries about a laundry service.

Eventually he picked us up and ferried us out to the camp site, 5 miles outside town and extremely difficult to find. The track was ill defined, full of deep pot holes, soft sand and one very steep drop of about four feet, which we never remembered during the following couple of days. The camping was excellent though; a clean tidy area in a pleasant grove of trees with immaculate showers and toilets—albeit with a murky cold swimming pool. A security guard patrolled the camp day and night and the French owner carefully checked all vehicles entering and leaving.

We cooked a belated supper, everyone almost past eating and in need of a good night's rest, and while David returned Susan and Sarah to their civilized beds, the boys helped me to organise the sleeping bags and in we thankfully climbed.

"Be quiet" I complained in more than a stage whisper. *"Oh what a beautiful morning, oh what a beautiful day"* sang two slightly out of tune polished English voices. "Rise and shine breakfast is ready, come on you lazy lot" cajoled the jolly leader of the big overland group next to us. It was only 6 o'clock! "I hope it chokes you!" I muttered ungraciously, pounding my pillow and dragging the blanket over my head, but further sleep was impossible. Gazing at the orange side of the tent; a deep glow spread slowly upwards from the ground as the sun woke up and stretched itself; and above the noisy clatter of the rising campers we heard a wonderful dawn chorus. The trees were full of little red-breasted, neat headed birds; only then did we realize how much we had missed the sound of birdsong during the past few weeks. It truly was a beautiful morning—and not to be wasted by lounging in bed.

The routine in camp always followed much the same pattern, showers and shampoos, catching up with the laundry, and service and clean our vehicle and equipment. Everyone including the children had their set chores and set about them quickly so that there would be time left to explore.

We had left most of the dirty clothes at the hotel laundry but the sail bag still contained a few miscellaneous evil smelling garments. I was getting quite adept with a scrubbing brush and stone slab by this stage and soon had them washed and drying in the brisk warm breeze. David and Peter disappeared underneath the Land Rover to check the oil level in the gear boxes. Sean tapped out sources of information about the next section to Zinder. We left Sarah and Susan to stroll lazily round the town searching for the post office and buying trinkets in the market.

Children clamoured round our tent trying to sell us tomatoes and carrots and marble sized potatoes. We quickly learned to halve the quoted price and then start bargaining from there. It was nice to taste fresh vegetables again. In the late afternoon we packed up as much as we could and drove the 5 miles back into town, David had booked supper at the hotel and we looked forward to a relaxed evening. The market place was humming with activity—and flies. The local Smithfield consisted of a number of large tables, spread with butchered meat of every description. Every tiny piece of the animal was displayed and for sale, and the children enjoyed a quick anatomy lesson as Susan pointed out the trachea and stomach and less attractive sections. The large flies hopped happily from table to table and then on to the bread next door.

One section of the square was set aside for brick making and another for a long collection of stalls selling silver trinkets and Tuareg daggers—all very highly priced but some quite beautiful. The people were a blended mixture of Arab and more negroid features and colouring. Many of the men wore tunic tops and trousers and the women gaily coloured scarves and robes, with babies slung over their shoulders. There was a general air of festivity and vitality notably absent in the silent Arab towns we had so far experienced.

As we walked back to the hotel in the twilight drums rumbled near by. Guided by the noise we groped up the tiny side streets in the sudden and always surprising darkness and watched a spontaneous dance and celebration in a narrow cul-de-sac. "I'm starving" said Susan, dragging us away and back to the hotel "I can't wait for supper a moment longer."

The dining room was delightful and the meal expertly cooked and served. We ate a delicious mutton couscous followed by salad and a caramel dessert. As his spoon clattered onto his empty plate, Sean put his head down on the table and promptly fell asleep. He was absolutely exhausted and of course it was way past our bed time, it was 9 p.m. We gathered up the sleepy children, collected the clean laundry and bundled them all into the Land Rover. David never managed to find the same route back to the camp on any two occasions. The compass direction was more or less right but we found ourselves driving into deeper and deeper soft sand and the familiar sound and feeling of spinning wheels dragged a weary groan from everyone's lips. We climbed out and prepared to push with little enthusiasm. A large off-white camel snorted and belched as it emerged from the darkness and its anonymous rider surveyed us silently from his aloof position. I approached him warily, keeping one eye on the camel's champing teeth. "Où se trouve le Camping?" I asked, peering up into the dark eyes and heavily veiled face. He pointed over to the right.

"Darling" I called to David, "there's a gentleman on a camel who says the camp is that way." Susan fell about laughing. "Oh no! I must add that to my collection of *treasured quotations while crossing Africa*" and she leant against the truck shaking and wiping away the tears as David joined in and teased me unmercifully.

With the family safely tucked up in the tent, we returned to the hotel. The shower was still cold but getting excited about it did not seem to make any difference, so we put up with it in resigned British fashion. It was a very musical bed we soon discovered climbing into the larger one, the slightest movement set the stretched springs twanging and bouncing in a very wild motion. The dip in the middle was like a trench and we rolled down on top of each other repeatedly with giggles from me and grunts from David. "I reckon the whole foreign legion has slept in this bed" he muttered, swinging out his legs and dragging back the grey looking sheets on the other one. We slept deeply and undisturbed, having a very desirable good night's rest.

Leaving Agadez next morning was a slow and frustrating business. Up early and out to the camp we had packed up the tent and beds and returned to pay the hotel bill but le patron was nowhere to be found. The police were grumpy and refused to release our passports for another hour and we hung around as the sun rose higher and the hours ticked by. Sean was delighted with the excuse for more time to play and stretched full length on the ground, elbow in the dust testing his strength against the local lads. He was surrounded by a large, admiring, laughing group who forgot momentarily to try to sell us good luck charms, swords and brittle peppery appetizers.

At last the hotel owner appeared and presented the bill. It was exactly double what we had expected. "Can the laundry really cost $8?" David asked me after a few quick sums and multiplications.

"Heavens no, I would have estimated about $4." He disappeared back into the hotel but reappeared with a grim face. Le patron would not budge an inch and refused even a small reduction to cover the lack of hot water as promised. We had learned the hard way.

Quickly buying a few loaves of bread from a nearby stall we left at last heading for what our notes promised us was the worst driving of the Sahara. The first 40 miles were reasonable on hard packed corrugated track, but this soon disappeared in favour of a maze of ill defined tracks in all directions with high central ridges and deep soft sand on either side. It was quite windy and wanting to make up some of our lost time we decided not to stop for lunch but have a 'meals on wheels'. I squatted in the back of the Land Rover and made large tomato sandwiches and shared out the flask of coffee. We nipped from one track to another as the first deteriorated and then on to another as the soft ridge stroked the belly of the Land Rover and threatened to drag us to a halt. The land was dead on either side, the few wisps of pale brown grass drooped in the sand. The white brittle thorn bushes were stripped skeletons, but still spiteful if we wandered too close. We watched the compass obsessionally; worried because we had not seen any main track for over an hour and our course seemed to be taking us deeper and deeper into the thorny jungle. "I think we'll look for a clearing and pitch camp" David suddenly announced. The children had been complaining of mild tummy pains and we did not want to try choosing a spot in the dark in this unfriendly wilderness. The thorns poked through our trousers, wriggled through our socks and tore our hands as we pulled the branches and broken bushes round three sides of the tent to give ample warning of approaching visitors. I peeled a mountain of tiny potatoes and made a pan full of chips as a special treat but as everyone seemed to be feeling slightly under the weather the treat fell flat. "Good night" "Good night" "Good night" echoed the three children as we settled down to sleep. I grasped the side of my camp bed as a severe pain gripped my stomach and threatened to tear me in two. I fumbled with the zip on my sleeping bag. "Quick Susie, pass me Sarah's bucket, I'll never make the door" I gasped. I vomited and retched and sobbed apologies to the rest of the family for about ten minutes before the spasm passed. Poor Susan spent a wretched night smoothing back my hair and wiping the sweat that trickled into my eyes as the spasms returned hour after hour.

David tossed and rolled in the far corner of the tent with similar pains but managed to fight off the nausea. Drifting off just before dawn, I slept deeply, oblivious of the activity around me. When I woke to the touch of a warm face cloth wiping my face, I saw that Susan and David had packed up the entire camp and were waiting to decant me into the back reclining seat all ready arranged with blankets and pillows.

Susan took over all the chores and she and David split the driving between them. I made no contribution to the day at all. The Piste, such as it was, could barely be distinguished, weaving in and out of the thorn bushes which became thicker and thicker as we moved south. The bland grass became confluent and slowly we drove into rolling country, climbing up and sweeping down into the next valley and then up yet another hill. There was a lot of very soft sand, deeply rutted and twice the sump bottomed and we were well and truly stuck. We had to unbolt the sand ladders and dig. Susan excelled herself, double de-clutching like an expert and slipping into low ratio as we wallowed and pitched along that impossible stretch. Two Volkswagen vans pulled up behind us, as we struggled yet again to scoop out deep channels for the ladders. We had seen them briefly the previous evening when they, like us, were searching for the Piste. Four strong German boys added their strength to ours and cheered us on our way.

Being a very unrewarding and bossy patient, I insisted on having a turn at the wheel as this would be our last day of desert driving. I rounded a corner. "Oh no" I exclaimed, a large trans-Saharan lorry was deeply bogged and slewed right across the track. "What are you going to do now my love" asked David, "you mustn't stop or we'll be in as deep as he is." I looked round wildly for another track but was out of luck. Taking a deep breath, I wound the wheel round to the right and like an ageing mountain goat we climbed hesitantly up the steep, soft side, swerved to miss an ugly looking tree stump and crashed back down onto the Piste behind the lorry.

"Just look how you girls have come along" he said rather patronisingly "five weeks ago that would have terrified you, stopped you dead in your tracks." Susan winked at me in the driving mirror; I gripped the wheel firmly to stop my hands shaking and made a mess of double de-clutching.

Twenty miles north of Tanout, we reached the end of the bad section. We had at last safely completed our Sahara crossing! Slipping a tape into the cassette player, we joined in a rousing tune, handed round the sweets and all felt very pleased with ourselves.

The firm bumpy corrugation felt reassuring as we quickly approached Tanout. On all sides we saw small groups of round grass huts and larger villages with mud houses. There were fields of tall dry brown plants which looked like millet and suddenly a lot of people everywhere. Slowing as we entered the town, only the children surrounded the Land Rover to sell us strong smelling cheesecake, their parents standing shyly back and watching from a distance. Rumbling on for a few more miles we chose a camp site on a slope overlooking the Piste and wound our way up to a group of sparsely-leafed trees. It only took nine minutes to put up the tent but a further hour to pick off the hundreds of 'sticky willies' which had barbs on their barbs and clung tenaciously to our pullovers and socks. David's watch stopped overnight so we all enjoyed an unofficial extra hour in bed, before he compared it with Susan's and chivvied us through a quick breakfast.

We wriggled and squirmed in our seats discovering more and more 'sticky willies', but forgot our discomfort momentarily as the corrugations smoothed out and a glorious stretch of tarseal lay before us. We made excellent time to the border and were delighted to meet up with a large overland group in a Bedford truck.

It took a few minutes to complete the form filling, everything in triplicate as usual, but the officials were easy going and after handing over a few antacid tablets for the chief's bad stomach, we left Niger and presented ourselves at the Nigerian customs and police post. What a relief it was to speak in English again after struggling for so long with our inadequate French; but entering Nigeria was a long and tedious business with lots of form filling and close scrutiny of documents. "What's the name of your children's school?" asked the policeman, pen poised. "Where does your wife work?" "What was your mother's maiden name?" He worked through his long list of questions and carefully checked everyone's health forms. Satisfied at last, he strolled out to the Land Rover and we held our breath. Please do not let him make us unpack it all everyone's eyes reflected. After no more than a cursory glance he stamped the carnet and passports and waved us through.

We checked the distance on the map, about 90 miles to Kano we reckoned. Regardless of time, we decided to keep driving until we got there. I made snacks and drinks on the move and we bowled along merrily, eating up the miles. There were people everywhere, hundreds in the villages and walking along the shoulder of the road. Vegetation increased on all sides and became more varied, large areas were cultivated and trees of many kinds became more and more abundant. It was quite nerve racking manoeuvring our way through one large village where a huge market was in progress. A large herd of oxen blocked the road and little boys ran backwards and forwards in front of us waving sticks and shouting at the bellowing animals. We had got out of the habit of looking in the driving mirror very often or giving any driving signals in the previous few weeks. There had not been anyone to signal to. We would have to mend our ways for town driving!

David took over as it grew darker and the children curled up for a sleep. We pulled up for a roadside police check and a charming young officer shook hands and welcomed us to Kano—we were at the outskirts much sooner than we had expected.

Everyone woke up, stimulated by curiosity and anticipation as the policeman offered us a guide to lead us to the campsite in the town. Unfortunately we had no Nigerian money and could not employ him. We drove confidently into the centre of Kano and were soon hopelessly lost in a maze of narrow little streets with foul-smelling open drains on either side and a heaving throng of people bustling among their dimly lit stalls. Bicycle riders wobbled dangerously near us and hand carts trundled across in front and behind. It was difficult to continue moving with safety and each street looked the same as the last. David grabbed a torch and jumped out to ask for some directions. I followed suit and managed to intercept a policeman. He could not have been more helpful. Swinging round his bicycle he pointed forward and with him pedalling rapidly in front we slowly followed for 10 minutes before he dropped it in a heap and pointed round to the right. We had nothing but cigarettes to offer in return for his kindness but he seemed well enough pleased as he pedalled off down the road.

It was dark and late. We put up the tent, had a quick meal and fell into bed.

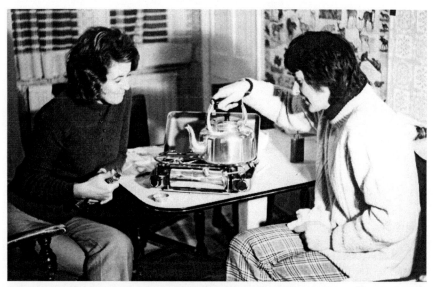

Before leaving, Maureen and Susan spent some time practicing the lighting sequence of the petrol stove. Despite their joint medical training, this stove was a perpetual challenge.

Publicity photo taken before departure.

Before leaving England to start the expedition we were warned that there were extremely muddy tracks through the jungle in the Congo basin and other areas in central Africa.
The heavy trucks that use these routes get so bogged down that they are sometimes stuck for weeks.
We practised driving slowly through deep water and soft sand in a quarry near Westerham in Kent.
In reality we found the soft sand in the Sahara sometimes just as challenging as the deep mud in Zaire.

Peter (in dark shirt) Sarah and Sean in good health in central Africa; desert boots already well worn.

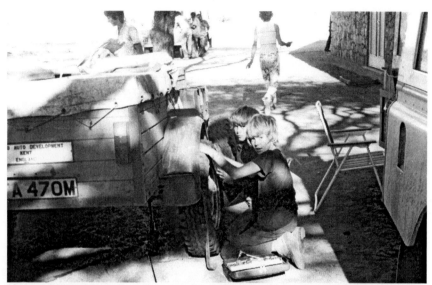

Peter and Sean working on the troublesome trailer wheel bearing in the shade, trying to get out of the heat. Their mum leaves them to it .

Before leaving England the boys were both given clip boards with a list of engineering checks that had to be made each day on the Land Rover and trailer ; some of these checks had to be carried out after the days run ; for example they had to check wheel bearing temperatures and let David , their father, know if one seemed to get hotter than the others.

During the first stop at Madrid when travelling down through Spain the Spanish press who gathered at the hotel ,were fascinated to see small children being given engineering responsibility of this type .

By the time the expedition started the Sahara crossing both boys were already fully familiar with all the expected oil pressure and temperature readings.

After many practice sessions at home in England the boys were expert puncture repairers; breaking the heavy tyre free from a Land Rover rim was no easy task for small boys.

The occasional oasis in the desert may appear a pleasant stopping place but also is seldom as clean as the open desert. Strangely enough if there are strangers around, security is also more of a problem, especially after dark.

Our Land Rover had a six cylinder low compression petrol engine and I had fitted a high voltage electronic ignition system in the Crayford factory before leaving. As a result the boys could kick-start the engine if needed.

Christmas 1974 found us celebrating in Tamanrasset in central Sahara. Our bearded friend we met a few days before with serious carburettor problems which we solved; temporarily.
The solution was for his partner to dribble petrol carefully through a stocking filter straight into the air intake; only possible because their vehicle had a forward cab layout with the engine partly in the cab. They were in effect driving a bomb.

Once in central Africa insects became more of a problem. We also sometimes found worryingly large paw marks round our camp at night. We often set up a trip wire surrounding our camp site; this was a thin wire about twelve inches from the gound that triggered the car horn if a strange animal decided to visit us. One morning we woke up to find lion sized paw prints in our camp site. We had been warned that the big cats will often attack the young of any species. They sense vulnerability.

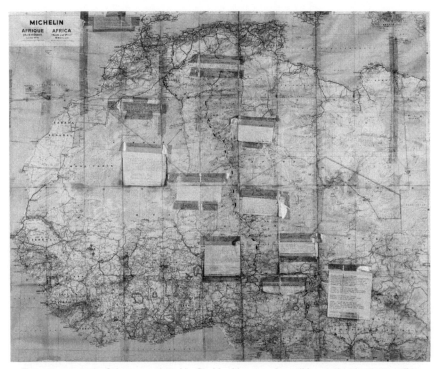

The route across the Sahara was plotted by David, with notes of possible petrol and water supplies

CHAPTER 7

KANO TO CAMEROUN . . .

THE RUMBLE GREW to a roar, wavering lights flashed haphazardly across the tent. A huge monster seemed to hurtle straight for us. David and I sat up in unison, my camp bed flipped and I lay in a struggling mass as a train pounded past. "Marvellous" I grunted "We've camped in the railway station, just what we needed."

Two hours later a large truck throbbed into life next to us. Low voices called through the darkness. I heard David groan and thump his pillow. "Mummy, Mummy, wake up" Peter and Sean knelt by my bed, eyes round in their serious faces, somebody died last night!" It was 7 o'clock. The boys had already inspected our new camp and were impatient with my reluctance to leap up and join them. "Where's the loo?" I asked them, zipping up my trousers and pulling on a dirty sweater. "We don't know, we went in the long grass" they called as they disappeared again. "Well I can't go in the long grass, not with all these spectators" I muttered, staggering out of the tent and viewing the many groups of campers.

David strolled back from one of the larger groups nearby, subdued and quiet. One of the young overlanders had in fact committed suicide during the night, hence the truck and noisy exchanges in the early hours. We inspected the camp site, with the railway line running along the edge and stacks of litter and rubbish in the grass. There was one tap, and a loo which did not flush if the tap was running—it was a great meeting place, there was always a long queue straggling round the local lorries parked for service and repair. Although a rather sordid site, tucked well away behind a splendid and expensive hotel the groups of young people we met were fascinating. We spent many happy hours listening to their adventures and David helped with their car problems.

"Fresh eggs?" asked a soft voice behind me, "Vegetables, fruit?" followed a chorus. The traders carried their baskets round the tents selling their wares which included fresh polythene wrapped bread, bananas and tomatoes. "Don't buy the eggs until I test them" called Susan, filling a bucket full of water. We gave three dozen the 'sink or swim' test before we selected twelve to our satisfaction, hoping the next customer would be as wise, as the trader tied our rejects into polythene bags and put them straight back on display.

Next door to the Central Hotel was the Kano Club, built by expatriates. For a very reasonable sum overlanders could have temporary membership and use their facilities which were excellent. There was a large swimming pool, showers, restaurant and iced drinks to order. David lost no time in paying our subscriptions and we wandered across the bumpy golf course with towels, swimsuits and sponge bags to clean up and lounge on the terrace. There was always a niggling anxiety about the safety of our belongings on the campsite so we either found a fellow camper willing to keep a wary eye open or else employed a guardian, by day and by night. He usually slept most of the night as far as we could see. More than once David shone a torch in his face in the hours before dawn, but he snored on happily.

We had further problems with the Land Rover and were in urgent need of repairs. Peter and Sean had noticed two days before reaching Kano that the ammeter was reading zero all the time. This meant we had a fault in the charging circuit and David felt sure it was a failure in the voltage control regulator. The trailer was also in trouble. The constant vibration had caused the springs to wear through the side walls of the shackles. We could not leave Kano until these problems were sorted out, for the further we progressed on our journey, the more difficult it became to find facilities and spare parts for repair—and ahead of us now lay the jungle of Equatorial Africa.

A tall, well built, aggressive Nigerian orbited round the site most of the morning offering his services as a mechanic and general repairs man but David did not take to him—felt he was 'all chat and no work' and was later proved right! We unhitched and parked the trailer and David went off to explore the town. He came back an hour later, well pleased with his trip. As always he had found a man who knew a man who might be able to help. He had also noticed not far from the camp a large branch of the British firm J. Lucas Ltd—they were very cooperative and quite prepared to strip and test the alternator and replace the control unit.

After two boiled eggs and fresh fruit for lunch—a rare treat and much enjoyed by everyone—the boys headed back to the pool while the rest of us piled into a taxi and went off for a guided tour of the town. We spent almost an hour wandering round the large market and through the little back street area we had seen the previous evening. Our taxi driver walked us through tiny shoulder-wide smelly alleyways between the booths, many selling beads, necklaces of agate and fabulous aromatic spices. We soon found it did not do to show too much interest in anything in particular, our guide would immediately drag us off to see a friend of his at another stall and start negotiating prices in the local tongue. He assured us he could guarantee us best value for money. We compared a few of his prices later and found they were sky high, fortunately we had just looked and not bought.

There was one large section of the market which throbbed with a steady rhythm of treadle sewing machines as yards and yards of brightly coloured cloth were transformed into trousers and tunics before our very eyes. It was a little sad to note on close inspection that the elaborate looking embroidery round the necks and sleeves was merely the zigzag and shell stitch I often did on my own home-sewing efforts and so the produce of different feet on the machine, and no longer the painstaking hand work of long ago.

Wandering down the side streets, we realized we must be in "Motor Town" as we stepped over hunks of twisted rusty metal and old bicycle frames stacked next to boxes of nuts and bolts. We picked our way cautiously over the open drains and round the many traders squatting in the dust and hot sunshine, each with an old tin in front of him filled with water. They frequently took a mouthful, blew it down their noses and then spat noisily into the dust beside them, pouring the remaining water over their heads. I almost wished I could do the same as the afternoon heat shrivelled us and wrung out the beads of perspiration leaving us dry mouthed and weak kneed.

On the way back to the campsite, the driver pointed out some of the twelve gates of the city and told us a little of the stormy history and new feeling in Nigeria. All in all it was a very worthwhile tour, our only complaint being the heat, but the locals assured us it was quite cold for them!

In clean clothes and with well scrubbed faces we strolled across to the Kano Club for supper. It was very good value. For $1 per head we ate lamb casserole and two veg' followed by sponge and custard, washed down with an excellent bottle of wine. Perhaps not having to fight with the petrol cooker made it taste twice as good. Tired and with the high hopes for a more restful night we climbed into our sleeping bags and settled down by nine.

"Give me the money, give me the money" screeched a female voice. David rushed out of the tent about midnight to see what was going on. A large group of Germans, high on drugs, were fighting with two local girls who had entertained them all evening and now wanted their dues. David left them to it. "Oh this glorious sexy camel" sang a loud inebriated English voice to the melody of the Eton Boating Song "Tra—la—la—la—la—la, wake up everybody, don't waste your lives sleeping." "No chance of that" groaned Susan, putting her pillow over her head. "We might as well stay awake until the train goes by" I suggested "and then it will be almost time to get up." We had all forgotten how noisy camp sites could be after our silent lonely nights in the desert. We thought of them with longing.

Morning came all too quickly. "I'll drop you in the town to do some shopping" David told me after breakfast. "I have to go to the garage to get the trailer welded." I hunted through my sail bag for a clean pair of jeans and quickly washed my hair in a bucket of cold water. "I want 190 Naira to the £1" David said firmly. I peered around through soap-filled eyes. The money changers were back, they were always hovering a stone's throw from the tents with bundles of notes in their hands. There was lots of thumb licking and mumbled counting. "I said 190" David thrust the handful of money back at the man. "I got 200" muttered an English lad as he walked past. This ritual of changing money was always a source of amusement and always ended up the same way. When they tried to short-change David, he would rapidly collect up all his own money, stuff it back in his pocket and tell them to come back tomorrow.

There were only four European type shops in the whole town. I strolled around the biggest, looking, believe it or not for a pair of rubber gloves to try to give my rough chapped hands a rest from cold water and detergent. The shop assistant was disinterested and waved a vague arm when I asked for help. The prices for everything were extortionate, most of the goods having been imported from England or the Far East. I settled for a flask and a pan scrubber, and seeing a European lady inspecting some tea cups I went over to her. "Excuse me; do you know if they sell rubber gloves in this store?" Chatting away in a soft lilting Welsh accent she guided me around the shop, but we had no luck. Mary was a charming woman, and when she learnt that we had come overland with our children, offered us the hospitality of her home. "Would you like a bath?" she asked us. I could not help smiling and thinking of the television advertisement 'Your best friend won't tell you' but I did not think I could be that bad. I warned her that there were six of us but she remained unruffled. "Meet me at the Kano Club at 6 o'clock" she instructed patting my arm reassuringly.

As I wandered round the food section, hastily closing my purse when I saw the price of a packet of Weetabix, I bumped into her once again. "I've just bought some meat she said" you must all have some supper with us."

Despite my protests she insisted. I could not wait to get back to the camp and tell the others. "What did you buy; anything nice to eat?" clamoured the children, unpacking my basket before I had time to put it down. "I've got a surprise for you all" I beamed. "I'm taking you out to supper—after a hot bath, of course." The children pulled a face, "Do we have to have a bath?" asked Sean ungratefully. David and Susan were delighted when they heard my news. The thought of being in a home again, if only for an evening, gave us all great pleasure. We dragged the hotel case down off the roof rack and put our 'best clothes' into a bag. We couldn't put them on until after our bath, but at least we would look respectable for supper.

At 6 p.m. we presented ourselves at the Golfers' Bar in the Kano Club. There was Mary, true to her word, looking cool and elegant and accompanied by her equally charming husband, Elwyn. They took us back to their beautiful home, tucked away in a quiet road and surrounded by multi-coloured flowering shrubs and shady trees. There was only one problem, explained Mary; the immersion heater only heated enough water for two baths, so we would have to share the water. We allotted one bathroom to the boys and the other to the girls and then tossed a coin for places in the queue. Susan and David were the unlucky ones, they won third place. But it was glorious in the hot water; this was our first bath since leaving Madrid five weeks previously. When everyone emerged shining and sweet smelling for cocktails in the lounge, Susan and I sneaked back into the bathrooms to look for the tin of Gumption and set to work on the tide marks!

We ate a delicious supper, complete with Xmas pudding which we had longed for and lost in the trailer mess. It was quite impossible to say a warm enough thank you to these kind and generous people. It had turned out to be one of those strange coincidences of life, while I had been chatting to Mary in the supermarket, David had been into Barclays Bank trying to negotiate money-changing and possible Telex arrangements, Elwyn turned out to be the Manager of Barclays Bank, so all our problems were solved. He gave us the full cooperation of the bank to send messages back home and change cheques.

The children spent every minute of our last day in Kano in the swimming pool, while David completed the repairs and servicing on the Land Rover, helped by a delightful young man called Solly. He had two young sons of his own and formed an instant attachment to Peter. "Where's my Peter?" was always his first question when he arrived. One morning he nipped across the railway line where work was in progress and reappeared a few minutes later pushing a bicycle he had just borrowed—

"For Peter to ride around on" he told us.

In the evening we had a date with Ted, manager of a brewery and a contact given to us by a friend in England. We sat down to the best Chinese meal of our lives in a restaurant exotically called the Pink

Peacock, and were mortified that we could not eat it all. The spring rolls and huge prawns were out of this world and we felt it was a mortal sin to have to walk away and leave half empty plates. We talked about it for the rest of the trip. Out in the car park, stomachs fit to burst; Ted loaded up our Land Rover with six crates of beer. We were to drink his health many times in the weeks to come and be grateful for his generosity more than once when a few bottles of beer saved the day.

We packed up expertly and quickly next morning, leaving a gaping hole in the line of tents and decided to spoil ourselves just once more before beginning the next leg of the journey. Waving goodbye to our many new friends, we pulled out of the camp drove down the road and swung right into the car park of the Kano Club. "Six double portions of bacon and eggs, two pots of coffee and plenty of toast" ordered David in the restaurant. We ate until not a crumb remained and eased ourselves out of the chairs. Now we could face anything.

After briefly stopping to say thank you again and goodbye to Mary and Elwyn, we left Kano on excellent roads. Despite our late relaxed start, we covered 160 miles. There were people and animals everywhere. The roadside was lined with clusters of well camouflaged woven huts with conical roofs, tucked in behind high fences and across the road. We braked and hooted and waved for hours on end! The land looked fertile and was well cultivated. Huge herds of oxen and goats grazed freely and donkeys galore trotted by with their large loads. Everywhere the vegetation was getting thicker and more luxuriant but all in varying shades of drab olive. We saw our first cotton fields, with little white puffs growing in profusion and then braked suddenly as another hen and her offspring tried to unsuccessfully fly in front of the Land Rover.

We stopped at about 4 p.m. when we had just about given up hope of finding a non-field, non-peopled, non-animal area. About a hundred yards off the road, we found a pleasant clean site amongst the trees, discreetly screened from passing traffic. David turned his attention first to the most important ask of cooling three bottles of beer by wrapping them in wet newspaper and leaving them in the warm sultry atmosphere—hoping the basic physics of evaporation and cooling worked. We decided on a simple camp, children in the

Land Rover in case of unwelcome wandering animals, and adults on camp beds, covered only by mosquito nets from the flying night life. We spent a glorious night under the African stars undisturbed by man or beast. In the early dawn we vowed, this was the life for us.

With so little gear to pack, we made an almost leisurely start to the day. Maiduguri was the next main stop according to the map and the roads looked good. This was our bird watching day. There were Magpies with extra long tail feathers and prolonged aquiline beaks and masses of gorgeous birds with Kingfisher colours but without the fisherman's beak. We thumbed through our books frantically trying to identify each one as the children looked and called out the markings. Kites soared lazily in the thermals and plump brightly coloured Spectators sat on the telegraph wires.

We reached Maiduguri by 3 p.m. with ample time to spare for exploration and relaxation. After many conflicting directions we found the campsite. With a most exquisite sense of humour the city fathers had placed it immediately next door to the Zoo! Enclosed in a high wire compound it was equipped with showers, fireplace, night guardian, a public footpath on one side and a cage full of Zebras on the other. Our fence was identical to those enclosing all the animals, and a crowd of grinning people quickly gathered, curling their fingers round the wire, watching us cook supper and listened to the children playing their guitars and singing. The night watchman smiled benignly as the children patted a seat and made room for him to join our sing song. In the public gaze, but dimmed by the descending darkness, we slept again under mosquito nets lulled by the high pitched laughter of the hyenas in the Zoo.

Leaving Maiduguri was a slow process. There seemed to be total confusion about custom offices and passport control, each one referred us to another office. Eventually we found that all controls had been transferred to a frontier village and headed off hopefully.

We left Northern Nigeria with a firm impression of a busy, prosperous and crowded nation, full of government offices, army posts, schools and training colleges—and people, people everywhere walking endless miles. As we approached the border, we saw ahead the lofty mountains and rolling grassy slopes of Cameroun. As usual all the forms were in triplicate but our exit was easy and without problems. A charming 12 year old called Aba seduced me with white toothed smiles and perfect English. He wanted English books to read. I rummaged through our book box, but could not really find anything suitable and finally gave him a block of paper and a box of coloured pencils. He was delighted but sad, he told me, because he had nothing to give me in return. I felt his twinkling eyes and happy smile were reward enough.

CHAPTER 8

WILL YOU STAY AND MARRY ME?

"IT'S LUNCHTIME" ANNOUNCED the Cameroun official as David approached him with our passports. He tipped back his chair and folded his arms. "When do you reopen?" asked David. The official shrugged his shoulders. "Perhaps in two hours." David walked slowly back to the Land Rover which was surrounded by a noisy jostling crowd of children. The temperature inside was already 95⁰ as the sun was beating down. Sean climbed out and patrolled the vehicle wagging his finger and shaking his head at the children as they tried to pick off the sticky labels and tugged at the lights. The two officials, one very overweight and sour looking, sat on their veranda and watched without a word. Every time we opened a window, a little hand popped in and made a grab at the nearest loose article. It was like sitting in an oven and being slowly roasted. Eventually I could stand it no longer. I walked slowly up to the veranda; pale, sweating and silent, clutching our documents. I smiled wanly, mopped by brow and held them out. We were cleared in five minutes! The impressions of eager black faces, lip marks and fingerprints were stamped though on every window of the Land Rover. Susan and I were always overcome with terrible feelings of guilt on these occasions. We had so much and these potbellied hungry children had so little. No wonder the odd one raised a fist and shouted. 'Tourist' or gathered up a handful of dust and gravel and threw it in our direction. It never angered us, only filled us with sadness and a terrible feeling of frustration.

Cameroun was a beautiful green, green country with rolling countryside and fields of crops with heavy mauve flowers. The huts were different, circular mud walls instead of thatch as in Niger and Nigeria, but with the same thatched conical roofs. Seeing no obvious campsite, we drove into Moroua, a lovely old French colonial town with tree-lined streets and deserted decaying houses with broken fences and wild sandy gardens.

David spoiled us. The first hotel was fully booked and did not want to know. After driving around for half an hour, we found a luxurious French owned, French run hotel, with beautiful bedrooms and en-suite bathrooms. There were bright red towels and sweet smelling soap, hot water galore and a delightful dining room. We all wallowed and simpered and promised we would ask for no more luxuries until the end of the trip. Madame was so sweet, but not so her prices, we shuddered next morning when we paid the bill, and were all especially nice to David all day.

The weather was very hazy and oppressive and we only had an impression of the beautiful hills and weird craggy rock formations. As always, people walked endlessly along the road side, stopping as we passed to look and wave and hold out their hands. They were beginning to look more primitive, bare breasted women with nose rings and a bony spike through their lower lips. Many of the men carried bows and arrows and raised them in a kind of salute as we rumbled past, leaving them enveloped in our inevitable trail of dust. Banana trees grew in abundance, and cotton fields lined the road and in a few areas it was stacked in huge snowballs, looking whiter than reality in contrast to the dark huts.

Disappointed by the weather and lack of visibility, we kept moving, except for stops to eat and stretch our legs until we reached South Cameroun and the area bordering on the National Reserve. We looked keenly and hopefully into the bushes, hoping to catch our first glimpse of wild animals, but at the end of the day had only chalked up one monkey and one snake.

Finding a suitable campsite posed quite a problem and we covered many extra miles before finding a tiny government camp not marked on the map. There was just one 'rondavell'—an African roundhouse—but already occupied by two French road surveyors, which had washing and lavatory facilities, and also a small grass hut, all watched over by a local family who lived nearby. They were so kind and helpful providing us with buckets of water and a hurricane light. Their children hovered shyly behind their parents, watching our every movement with wide serious eyes, hands clasped round their pot bellies. There was no fixed rate for camping so we worked out what we considered a reasonable figure and added beer and matches for Dad and sweets for the children. We were very comfortable, Susan and David and I slept at the side of the Land Rover again with only the mosquito nets—they always gave a false feeling of protection. We put the three children in the grass hut to be on the safe side—dense jungle was only a few yards away. Lying in the darkness, the stars blotted out by the still heavy low lying cloud, we listened to the jungle noises and tried to identify them, without much success.

Only the faintest haze lingered in the early morning. The air was fresher and clearer and we were able to see much more of the lovely countryside as we climbed into the Massif on narrowing roads and round hairpin bends. The tarseal petered out and was replaced by bumpy track liberally covered by thick layers of rich red dust which rose in clouds around us and filtered through every crack. It clung to our hair and eyebrows and streaked our faces like war paint as we wiped damp sticky hands down our cheeks. For the first couple of hours, the track was filled with people walking, walking endlessly, to school, to the next village, to who knows where. They parted like the Red Sea, melting into the bushes on either side as we passed.

After steadily plodding on for most of the morning, we reached N'Goundere, a fairly large spreading town. While David filled up with petrol, Susan and I went in search of the post office to buy stamps. We walked slowly up the wide streets, stopping to poke our heads into tiny shops selling materials, handbags and poor quality carvings. The post office was the usual hive of industry, with no apparent queue system.

"Oh Mummy, look!" laughed Sean as we headed off again. Stepping out onto the road, a large ox raised its head to the sky and with quivering nostrils called to the rest of the herd to follow. They meekly obeyed, quickly disappearing from sight on the other side while Susan and I sat shamefaced and laughing with relief. Our unscheduled stop had made us rather late; we had hoped to reach the border but it was out of the question now. We combed the dense trees and bushes on either side as we drove along, looking for a clearing suitable for camp but found none. We began to appreciate that our camping problems had just started. We had taken for granted the freedom of the desert, the miles of open space always available for pitching tents. Spreading and smoothing the map, we pinpointed a small place called Meiganga. There was a little sign next to the name indicating a camp site. We drove hopefully towards it, but I shook my head when the owner of the local beer house pointed to a dirty scrubby patch at the back of his establishment, watched by two giggling teenagers who had taken a fancy to David. It would have taken hours to clear away the smelly litter and empty beer bottles, and fit ear plugs to drown the noise of the jolly customers. Every one was tired and a little dejected. "We'll just have to bowl on" David said as we all climbed aboard again, hot, dirty and rather silent. After a quick tour round the village and a few enquiries about a hotel we gave up and headed out on the road to the border.

Sarah banged her head and shouted with pain as David suddenly swung sharply to the left up a bumpy tree lined avenue. We slowed to a halt in front of a low rambling down-at-heel house with rickety outbuildings and scattered junk, all enclosed by a tall wire fence and closed gate. A faded sign advertising the presence of a club hung motionless in the heavy humid atmosphere. "You go in and have a look darling" said David slumping wearily in his seat. I mentally crossed my fingers as I undid the string round the post and walked up to the door. It was opened before I had time to knock by a fat, pasty-faced old Frenchman. His chest rose and fell rapidly as he inhaled shallow lungful's of air and blew them out again through pursed bluish lips to an accompanying squeaky wheeze and final high pitched whistle. His square, puffy nicotine-stained hand gathered up a stray lock of greasy grey-streaked hair and swept it back across his forehead. I launched into my best French as I followed him into a large dim room, at one end of which was an old sideboard and a group of faded bulgy armchairs, and at the other a long table covered with a white stained tablecloth and a few scattered place mats. He puffed and rolled slightly from side to side as he walked ahead to show me the bedrooms, talking quickly and indistinctly in husky French. It was all far from salubrious but adequate. If we unpacked two camp beds we could manage with two rooms and share the bucket shower. I stuck my head out of the window and gave David the thumbs up sign.

Throwing ourselves thankfully into the armchairs, our eyes lit up with renewed enthusiasm when Le Patron produced cold beer and squash for the children. The beer seemed very strong. Susan and I felt quite light headed and laughed too loudly as we went off to sort out beds and clothes, leaving David to have another.

The dirty laundry bag was swollen, crammed with hard smelling socks, filthy jeans and shirts. The bathroom was not ideal for laundry but by filling bowls from the tap at the basin and getting down on our hands and knees on the concrete floor, we could scrub the clothes on the wooden slats in the depression of the shower. Peter lit the hurricane lamp and put it next to the lavatory and the three children watched in amusement as Susan and I stripped down to bra' and pants and began scrubbing and patting the soggy clothes with new found energy and much hilarity. "Ask Daddy if we can have another beer" I instructed Sarah, pushing back a loose strand of hair with a soapy forearm. She returned five minutes later. "Daddy wants you to come and meet the local police chief and his friends, they are all having a drink together." "We'll all be locked up if I appear like this" I laughed, catching sight of myself in the speckled old mirror. "Tell him I have to finish the washing."

Le Patron cooked the supper himself as one of his 'boys' was sick and the other in prison. He refused my offer of help in the kitchen but reluctantly allowed the children to set the table. Each time he limped and wheezed past, he paused to top up his glass from a bottle of red wine and puff his drooping cigarette. He was obviously a very lonely man, glad of the opportunity to talk. As he served us soup and delicious cheese and onion omelettes, he kept up a continuous somewhat incoherent monologue of his early life, when he had fought in North Africa and displayed his shrivelled scarred arm when he relived the Normandy Landings. It was difficult to get away to bed. He pulled the cork out of another bottle of wine, pulled up a chair and joined us over our coffee, working himself up into an indignant frenzy at the lack of responsibility and patriotism of modern youth.

David and I had a dreadful night. Susan refused to sleep with Sean in her room because of his unendearing night time habits. He shouted, ground his teeth and created a stink at the first buzz of a mosquito. By the morning David refused to sleep with him again either.

Before leaving we topped up our water carrier and secretly crept out with our large bag of wet washing. In front of the gate was the most beautiful tree—a type of palm but not like any other I had ever seen. It had no depth, no impression of any third dimension. I was sure it was cardboard, and refused to leave before I dashed across to touch it, while everyone sat impatiently in the Land Rover, anxious to be away. We wanted to avoid another lunch time session at the border if possible, our entry into the country had not left us feeling altogether welcome.

David went in with the children to collect the usual bundle of forms for completion. Peter emerged a few minutes later. "Daddy wants you to go and help him" he told me. "What's the problem?" I asked quietly as David came to the door to meet me. "Nothing special, but the atmosphere feels a bit tense in there, see what you can do." I went into the office and looked at the group of miserable looking Africans sitting handcuffed on the floor. The officer regarded me silently and stony faced. I put on my brightest smile and walked forward with outstretched hand. "What a busy morning you seem to be having, and now we have arrived to add to your work! I do hope my children didn't get in your way. If you could just stamp our passports, we'll move along and leave you to more important matters" I pattered on, opening the passports and putting each one in front of him in turn. He smiled bleakly, handed me back the bundle and wished us "Bon Voyage." "From now on you approach all the customs and police" David told me as we started up the engine "I never thought you'd be able to wring a smile out of that one."

We stopped in 'no-mans' land for another hot uncomfortable roadside lunch. Dragging down the bag of wet clothes, we hung them gypsy fashion on the bushes and low branches. They were only half clean and many had long brown stains across them where the dye from the wooden-slatted floor of the shower had run and oozed into the material. The mellow light from the hurricane lamp from the night before had lulled us into a false state of efficiency.

Drawing to a stop at the customs post into Central African Republic David sat back and folded his arms. "Women and children out, go and do your bit girls." He handed me the bag containing all our paper work. The chief, a tall slim good-looking young man remained seated at his desk as we entered the small room. His eyes examined us closely as he stretched out a hand for our documents. He turned the pages slowly and thoughtfully. "You're not married?" he said to Susan in precise, clear French. "No I'm not" she replied. There was another long pause. "Will you stay and marry me?" he asked with a straight face. I grinned and looked expectantly at Susan, waiting for her witty reply. She was completely taken off guard, colouring slightly and laughing nervously. "I haven't had time to see your country yet" she said side-stepping the question. "We'll look at it together" he replied as he continued to turn pages and bring down his rubber stamp with a crash. "I feel I ought to continue the journey with my friends." Susan's eyes implored me to join in the conversation, but I sat in amused silence listening to the unlikely dialogue. "That's easy, I'll come with you" he replied with a growing twinkle in his eye and a slight twitch of the lips as he handed me back the passports. "It will mean travelling with three children." Susan felt this must put him off. "I like children, I hope we will have many more than three." The chair scraped on the floor as he stood up and towered over us. "You still haven't answered my question, will you marry me?" We got to our feet. Susan shrugged her shoulders and spread her hands in a doubtful gesture. "I'll need time to think about it. I'll have to let you know." We all shook hands and laughed. We were half way down the stairs when he called us back. "If you won't marry me, be my doctor, I have a bad stomach." I dug in my bag and found half a bottle of soluble Aspirin. I handed them to Susan and beat a hasty retreat, leaving her to explain the dose and tidy up her marital affair.

The road became noticeably worse, with deep ruts and very dusty, but now narrow-ridged and potholed, marching indomitably across range after range of hills, up and down like a giant switchback. We met the first of many unfenced plank bridges across bilharzia-infested streams and found it slightly unnerving as our heavily laden truck and trailer clattered and rumbled across. A small branch snapped under our wheels as I drove round a bend, only to slam on the brakes and slither to a halt. The road fell away, with a sheer drop into the river bed below. The broken bridge lay in jagged pieces on the rocky slopes. We climbed out and surveyed the area on foot. The branch across the road had obviously been put there to indicate a diversion, and we found a little-used but safer track leading across the river further down. "Whew, thank heavens it wasn't dark and we saw that one in time" I muttered, backing slowly and driving down the secondary track.

The jungle grew thicker with tall trees strangled by creepers pressing in on the road. There was nowhere to camp. We decided to drive all night and make for the capital Bangui. The entire population of C.A.R. seemed to live along the roadside, strung out in endless small unfenced villages. Their rectangular mud houses were decorated with symbols and blotches of white paint, and their goats, pigs and pullets wandered in and out across the road.

We stopped in a small clearing to cook a meal before beginning the long night drive. Within minutes we were surrounded by a chattering throng of walkers who pointed at us and laughed at every thing we did. We must have made a very strange spectacle with our table, pans of sausage and mash and vast collection of bits and pieces. We parked the children on top of the open trailer to eat their supper as darkness fell. There were so many people around us we couldn't keep an eye on all our equipment at the same time and felt that some might mysteriously disappear. We gathered together all our pieces of foam and spread them in the back of the Land Rover together with blankets and sleeping bags for the children. They climbed in and happily wriggled and snuggled together. We split the driving into hourly shifts. It worked very well with three people. One hour as driver, followed by an hour resting and dozing in the reclining seat and the next as co-driver, chatting to the driver and getting used to the road conditions again.

The night sky glowed and flickered from the blaze of numerous bush fires—many extending to the roadside and quite frightening to drive through. We learnt later that they were started intentionally by the villagers to clear the ground but often became totally out of control. The acrid smoke and fumes from the blackened charred vegetation stung our nostrils and mixed with the ever-present red dust clouds, irritated our eyes and wrung out involuntary tears. We paused and stopped and stared at each precarious looking bridge, while the children slept, oblivious of our growing fatigue and shortening tempers. Wild life was non-existent, except for the owls which seemed to enjoy sitting in the road blinking into our headlights and two rabbits which hopped blindly and irrationally in front of us.

At 7 a.m. we reached the outskirts of Bangui and crashed off the road among a pile of felled trees. The children were full of beans, having rested and slept quite well and only had one thought in their heads—food. David, Susan and I took a deep breath of the early morning air and straightened our drooping aching shoulders. Our hair was wild, standing up in red dust-covered tufts; lines of grime surrounded our puffy strained eyes. We dragged out the cooker without much enthusiasm and put on a kettle and a pan of water to boil. Our clothes were beyond redemption. No amount of brushing would remove the thick lines of dirt which marked the legs of our trousers where they had folded in sweaty, moist creases during the night. I surveyed our caked sandaled feet and dragged out a small bowl from the trailer. Silly the things that seemed to matter in that zombie state of fatigue. David watched with exasperated exclamations as I washed and scrubbed my toes. I wouldn't leave until I felt that we were half presentable.

Although Bangui is only a large city, as the capital of C.A.R. it demands separate entrance and exit customs and police formalities. It was weary women and children who smiled weak smiles at the officials and filled in forms with aching fingers.

We drove down the wide busy streets lined with universities, schools, colleges and hospitals and watched the well dressed population fight with their morning rush hour. We stopped for directions, were moved on by the police and did a complete circuit of the city before we found the French Protestant Mission which offered excellent and hospitable camping facilities for overlanders.

Instead of camping in the grounds of this modern, beautifully equipped boys' boarding school, we hired one of their two visitors rooms. Built in concrete with high ceilings and no windows facing anything but the early morning sun, it was cool and airy. The only furniture was six beds with mosquito nets and a table, absolutely ideal. Next door were basins, lavatories and showers. We flung ourselves on the bouncy beds while the children splashed and squealed in the showers. We felt like going to bed but it was only 11 a.m. We promised each other an early night.

I stayed behind in this welcome oasis and confess that I drifted into a dreamless sleep while David and Susan went off to investigate the town—and find the post office, for Susan of course. The mission boys arrived back from school and kept the children well occupied while I shamelessly slept, sprawled in a most unladylike fashion.

We planned a one day stop before moving on, but our hands were tied by red tape. Susan and David returned with a basket of fresh fruit and tales about visa requirements. We decided that cooked hot lunches in the temperatures we were now suffering were ridiculous. From then on we would eat fruit and cheese and biscuits, falling back on our tinned fruit when no fresh fruit was available.

Refreshed and revived, Susan and I headed for the washroom and scrubbing board with armfuls of dirty clothes while David went back into town to sort out the paper work and passports. As I rinsed and pounded the dust-stained clothes, Sarah rushed in and grabbed me round the legs.

"He wants to marry me" she gasped, pink and coyly fluttering her eyelashes. "Who does?" I filled up the sink for yet another rinse. "That big boy, out there, talking to Sean." She grabbed my legs tighter and giggled as a handsome sixteen year old came into the washroom and turned on a tap. He whipped up a lather with a handful of detergent and threw in his jeans and shirt. "That one" she whispered, and dashed out. He pounded and rubbed his clothes—all the boys at the mission did their own washing. I surveyed him over the top of the partition. "So you want to marry my daughter" I teased him keeping my head down and scrubbing furiously.

"Is she yours?" he stumbled in embarrassed French. "Are you her mother?" I hoped he meant I looked too young but I suspect he thought I looked too old. "It was only fun" he explained. "We were just having fun." "She's only eight" I told him, "You will have to wait until she is sixteen, that's the law in England." "Tell me about England" he implored me. "Do you have schools like this, do your children wash their own clothes? "I wish they did" I replied, picking up another pair of stinking socks "I think you could teach them a thing or two." We laughed and joked as we pegged out our washing on the line in the hot sunshine. Sean appeared with his guitar and a group of boys gathered round to sing and clap. I was happy to see them all mix so well and have fun together.

David returned rather tense and white-faced. It had been quite an afternoon. At the police and immigration office he had bumped into another English group, who were camping in the mission grounds but in their two weeks of residence had not found out about passport requirements. "Stupid, black, pig faced, gits" yelled the Englishman ahead of David in the queue. David's skin prickled and felt icy cold in the hot little office. "Stamp our bloody passports and stop messing about" he bawled, standing hands on hips and glowering at the officer. His friends stood close behind to give moral support. David watched and listened in mortified silence as the office filled with African officials. They pushed and jostled the offending group down the steps and out into the courtyard. "We shall withhold all British passports because of your insolence and disrespect" the boss called after them as they departed with further abuse and rude gestures. David stood there with our bundle of passports in his hand, looking at the impassive faces and angry eyes of the African officials. On a sudden inspiration he dashed down to the Land Rover, unpacked a crate of beer and staggered back up the steps. He placed his clinking, jangling olive branch on the steps at the feet of the officials, apologizing on behalf of his countrymen, and handed over our passports.

We woke up refreshed and ready for anything the next morning. "I think I may need the feminine touch" David told me as I back combed my hair and blotted my lipstick. "I'd like to get our passports back this morning. Come and see what you can do—bring the children they always help." We drove down through the wide tree-lined streets with cool white buildings on either side. Red and purple splashes of heavy blossom blended with the colourful dresses of the women with their strange spiky, plaited hairdos, sticking out like crazy wireless aerials. We rushed up the steps into the small airless office, followed hot foot by the offensive group from the evening before. We parked our bottoms on a row of bleached uncomfortable white wood benches and waited. I had primed the children to put on their best smiles and not to show any impatience or poor manners. As soon as anyone appeared looking official or in any way important, we rose to our feet, shook hands and exchanged polite courtesies. The group next to us growled and muttered. An hour and a half later the boss beckoned us forward to his desk. The group sitting next to us rose to their feet. "Sit down" the customs officer said politely but firmly in French, pointing at them. They cursed and grumbled, slumping back with crossed legs and folded arms. With everyday pleasantries and smiles we were handed our stamped passports and visas and stepped out into the hot sunshine.

"We intend to hold your passports" the official explained to the remaining group as we left, "to teach you a little respect." "Speak in bloody English" their leader retorted, "I know you can." "We are a French speaking country" he replied, "our business is conducted in French. You must address your requests and enquiries in French."

They followed us down the steps. "I think you have been very rude and offensive to these officials" said David in a typically British understatement, "but is there anything we can do?" "Get stuffed" snarled the eldest man. I saw David stiffen, "I hope to God I don't have to follow you around Africa, man, you spell nothing but trouble." He climbed in, started the engine and reversed rapidly out of the courtyard.

There were still further customs' requirements. Instead of driving on through C.A.R. we had decided to take the ferry across the Oubangui River straight into Zaire. Just as we arrived at the customs office they closed their doors for a two hour lunch break. "I'll treat you all to a cold drink" said Susan, "let's find somewhere on the banks of the river." David organised a fisherman to take him and the children out in a dugout canoe, while Susan and I indulged in very expensive drinks on the veranda of a hotel. We returned to the mission and spent a couple of hours reorganising things in our dusty, dirty trailer before settling down to an early night in bed.

After a quick breakfast of dry bread and black tea with the boys at the mission, we presented ourselves at the ferry at 7.30 a.m. as instructed, only to find that the engine had broken down. Undaunted, David ditched us in the local market place to buy bread and fresh fruit, and set off to negotiate with nearby navy tugs. An hour later a naval barge chugged up the river, prepared to push the ferry across the river to the opposite bank. We groaned though as we approached the slipway. There stood the Range Rover with the aggressive unfriendly English party and behind them a Land Rover with two young adopted friends! We lined up and were followed by an orange Volkswagen van driven by a young German couple—Doris and Hubert—with their two year old son Armine bouncing up and down in his mother's arms.

The captain signalled our Land Rover down the slope onto the ferry, but waved his arms frantically when the other Range Rover tried to follow. They backed disconsolately up the slope and scowled as we rolled down and edged our way onto the ferry—but let's face it, David had made it possible. "We can't talk to them" I said to David as the boat made ready to set out on its way across the river. He walked forward and I saw him bend down and chat to the English family and then shake hands. Susan and I heaved a sigh of relief. None of us liked emotional tensions.

CHAPTER 9

ONWARD CHRISTIAN SOLDIERS . . .

WE APPROACHED ZAIRE with a lot of apprehension through the early morning haze. In the campsite at Bangui we had listened to a horrifying tale about a German couple who together with their young baby had been held prisoners the previous week, in a small village, miles from anywhere. They had been threatened with death, baby first, or so the tale went. We did not know what to expect.

The run off the ferry was challenge enough. There was no fixed track. The bank was steep, sandy and soft. We inspected it carefully before David took the plunge, selecting low ratio and putting his foot flat on the boards, while we watched with bated breath. He made it in one fast dashing run up to the rough road.

There was a long queue at the customs post, mostly of women with large loads strapped on their heads and backs. An old emotionless Zairen collected the customs dues for their goods being imported across the river. They haggled and threw their hands up in despair, but he held out his hand silently and dispassionately, and could never find any change in his loaded bulging pockets. "How much Zairen currency have you got?" the customs officer asked David. "None" he replied. "How much foreign currency have you got, then?" I held my tongue. David quoted a low figure and the officer insisted on changing it into local money at his own rate. We left with no further problems and two notes worth $10. The police were charming and wished us a happy journey through their country.

We crashed and rolled along the narrow track with heavy deep green tropical growth on either side. Tall willowy grass filled the gaps between the palm trees and the villagers waved cheerfully and with friendly smiles. We relaxed, there did not seem any cause for anxiety. We drove about 40 miles before stopping to squat on the lush verge and eat a light lunch.

"We must get some pictures of the Land Rover being driven along this jungle lined track" said David, getting out his cine and polishing the lens. "I'll walk on and round the corner, you take your time packing up and drive slowly towards me" It was too hot to rush. We wiped up the sticky remains of the fresh pineapple, filtered another large container of cold water and took up our new driving position. It was hot and humid and we all felt very lethargic. As I rounded the corner we all gasped as one. A large army truck blocked the track. It shunted and reversed to complete the obstruction as we appeared. David was standing white faced, surrounded by a group of angry shouting soldiers, arms pinned to his side as another dragged the camera strap over his head. He was speaking quickly, nervously in a slightly higher tone than normal, trying to explain that he was just taking family pictures. No-one wanted to listen. "Your women and children will go back as well" yelled the boss man, "You will be interrogated." "Daddy, Daddy, don't you touch my Daddy" shouted Sarah, clenching her fists and pounding the back of the seat. "Relax, relax, kids" I soothed, "remember your manners and your French. Come on everybody, smile and don't forget to shake hands." I felt sick and swallowed hard. Three or four of the soldiers sauntered across to us, we stuck our arms out of the windows and shook hands firmly. "Would you like a sweet?" asked Sean smilingly angelically. He handed round a tube of pastilles. One soldier reached in and pinched Sarah's cheek, Susan and I smiled and chattered, wiping sweaty palms down the legs of our jeans and fighting off the rising nausea. David opened the passenger door of the Land Rover and dug out the Polaroid camera, demonstrating its qualities with expert salesman's flare. The boss was not impressed. He rubbed his thumb and forefinger together and held out his hand behind the cover of the half open door. "He wants money" I told David, quickly understanding the well known gestures. I pulled up my shirt and unzipped my money belt, handing our only Zairen money to David. Not enough, indicated the soldier, holding his hand out for more. We felt quite desperate; we did not have any more! David had a sudden flash of inspiration. "Would you like some beer?" He asked them including the whole group and not just the slick money grabbing boss man. Their faces broke into smiles. He dashed round to the other side of the Land Rover, untied the roof rack cover and unloaded one of Ted's crates. "Get the engine ticking over" he told me hoarsely, "You should make it round those tree stumps if you are careful." We sat there with fixed smiles as the Land Rover throbbed reassuringly. David flipped the tops off a couple of bottles, swopped one for his cine camera and climbed into the passenger seat. "Bon Voyage, happy days" we called as they fell on the rest of the crate and we crept slowly forward. "Don't rush and keep waving" instructed David in a tight voice. We left them to their celebrations, not daring to stop to relax our shaking limbs. Our apprehension about the forthcoming journey was increased tenfold.

In the middle of the afternoon the orange Volkswagen van we had first seen at the ferry caught up with us. We conferred with Doris and Hubert about a communal camp that night while Armine gurgled and showed off to our children. We drove in convoy, hopefully looking for a clearing but our efforts were unrewarded. The sun went slowly to bed and exchanged its intense heat for a dull heavy stillness. We had to stop driving soon. "How about taking pot luck in one of these villages?" asked David, as we drove along through the ever present roadside population. Susan and I had not forgotten the experience earlier in the day, I squeezed her hand. "No harm in trying" I replied brightly. The children continued to wave to the continuous line of Africans who moved from their huts with outstretched hands and hopeful faces. We slowed down and stopped. The Volkswagen drew abreast. Hubert and Doris did not speak one word of French and sat in silence while the villagers crowded round and David tried to communicate with them. He had seen a clearing next to a large hut which turned out to be the church. One bright young man stepped forward to help. He spoke fluent French, learnt at the Catholic Mission School, which he had attended until the age of 17.

A dear old lady, the Ena Sharples of Zaire, with short crinkly grey hair and a toothless smile poked her head through the open window of the Land Rover. She pointed at the children and cackled; Sean gave her a big wink and stretched out his hand. As she dragged on his arm, he slipped open the door and jumped down out onto the dusty road. With his arm firmly tucked through hers, she with her shrivelled pendulous breasts swaying round her waist, they did a spontaneous music hall 'We'll walk down the avenue' turn, much to the delight of the watching villagers. We were in! The senior man signalled us to pull across the road onto the bare patch next to the Church and together with the Volkswagen we arranged a small square compound, watched closely by children and grandmothers, youths and wise old men. Vincent, the French speaking 20 year old, acted as interpreter and go-between. He told us that the chief would visit us later.

"Psst" he beckoned, though, with his finger, and I went round to the back of the Land Rover. "Have you got any Benzedrine?" he asked me. I was horrified and backed away as I shook my head. "Psst" he repeated, calling me back and opening his hand carefully to reveal an empty intravenous injection bottle. "Have you got any?" he pleaded. I felt slightly sick, I could not really believe it, here in a remote little village! I just stood there shaking my head and started to unpack the food for supper. Armine lightened the atmosphere, pushing his small plastic wheelbarrow in and out of the legs of the gathered throng so that they leapt shrieking to one side as he wheeled and turned and made an even more determined effort to get them next time.

As we sat down to eat, everyone suddenly melted away and we were left with the gathering jungle noises and scrape of forks on plastic plates. The village allowed us a respectful half hour for supper before girlish giggles from the Church told us that they were back and watching us again. A rather bumptious, forceful young man appeared and introduced himself as the political guardian. He was closely followed by the chief, an elderly, wizened, silent man, whose every word and move seemed to be dictated by his young companion.

We arranged the seats round in a circle, opened a few bottles of beer and handed round the cigarettes. Sean climbed up onto the roof rack and lifted down the two guitars. After a few minutes tuning and twanging, the children began their entertainment. The villagers applauded enthusiastically but the chief sat with dull unresponsive eyes, drinking his beer. "What about singing something in German for Doris and Hubert?" suggested David. The children only knew one German song, 'Stille nacht, Heilige nacht'. Both families joined in. A flicker of a smile suddenly crossed the chief's face. "That's it" exclaimed David "he'll know some hymns that they sang in the missions. Try and play some hymns, boys." Peter and Sean rolled their eyes and looked at me in desperation. "Onward Christian Soldiers" I sang lustily, as the boys strummed the tune quietly. I wished we had Sarah's hymn book that David had firmly removed from the book box before we left, feeling it was unnecessary weight. We struggled through another couple, but the chief was beginning to enjoy himself, and held out his empty glass for a refill.

Sean had learnt two special African handshakes from his numerous friends along the way, different ways of clasping the hand and curling the thumb round. He walked over to the chief, held out his hand and tried them. The old man was delighted and cackled loudly showing his sparse yellow teeth as he ruffled Sean's hair. Sean pulled up a chair next to his new conquest and with grubby fingers peeled an orange and broke it into sections. As we all watched with slack jaws, he popped the segments one after another into the chief's mouth, chattering away and laughing as they both shared some private joke.

David had a talk with the political guardian and arranged for two night guards to watch over us. We had a lot of valuable equipment scattered around and of course the jungle was only a few feet away. The villagers and the guards built a large fire close by and prepared for their long vigil. Their price was one packet of cigarettes in advance and two more in the morning.

"What do you think the drums are saying?" I whispered to David as we lay listening to their steady hollow rhythm. "Heaven knows, probably watch out for guitar playing, sticky orange fingers or something." The steady beat continued long into the night accompanied by high pitched squawks and muffled bellows from the jungle.

As we drank our coffee in the noisy twittering dawn, Sean's old lady friend hovered around our camp. She patted and stroked him and he showed her around the Land Rover leading her by the hand.

Sarah rubbed sleepy eyes and ate her cereal unenthusiastically while Susan fought the inevitable battle with the petrol stove, which as usual spluttered and spat at her with unrelenting bad temper. David clambered up and down onto the roof rack, stacking away all our gear. It still took well over an hour to get us on the road and David always felt quite exhausted by the time we started after all the packing.

Hubert and Doris still had to feed Armine so we left them and promised to meet up later for lunch. Their unit was much more compact than ours. They slept in the van with Armine happily slung in a hammock in the driving compartment and they therefore carried much less equipment than us. When their wheels were rolling they travelled much faster too.

As we waved goodbye to the villagers we all wished we could have stayed longer with them and learnt more about their daily life and community. In the cool of the early morning the families huddled round small fires in front of their huts, but as the sun broke into a broad smile, the men stretched out on benches and old ragged deckchairs and prepared for another long sleepy day. Old women staggered along the roadside carrying heavy loads of wood, tied in a bundle and supported on their backs by a thick strap across their foreheads. Young women with their babies slung on their backs, washed clothes and walked miles to collect water and food. We began to feel in total sympathy with our Royal Family as we waved and smiled hour after hour driving through the villages. Children and adults all stood with outstretched hands and even tiny tots raised two fingers to their mouths and made a gesture of smoking. They all wanted cigarettes.

We were still driving south, getting nearer and nearer to the River Zaire; we felt it's old name the Congo sounded more romantic but perhaps we had seen too many films. The humidity increased steadily and the temperature rose to 100^0 in the Land Rover. This was our first truly uncomfortable day. Even the towels which we spread over the backs of the seats were soon wet and smelly from our freely perspiring bodies. It really was hot!

The dense heavy vegetation was splashed with colour. Beautiful wild poinsettia spread their elegant red petals up to the sun and bougainvillea wound its way round matted branches. Some bushes sported large yellow trumpets and the vulgar purple banana blossom hung beneath shiny jagged leaves. The most glorious sight of all was the butterflies, thousands and thousands of the most exotically coloured butterflies we could ever imagine. They collected in moving eye-startling rainbows over the murky little streams, very large swallow-tailed ones in emerald or peacock and edged with black, smaller yellows and oranges and pretty little violet treasures with brown underbellies. They were a constant source of pleasure and amazement to us all.

A small group of children wandered down the road followed by an old man as we stopped to eat in a shady spot. One carried a homemade musical instrument which he plucked with his fingers. We shared out the remains of our lunch with them and asked them to play and sing for us. David switched on the tape recorder. Some sang, some giggled and some made what were obviously saucy remarks judging by the reaction of the old man. David flicked the switch on the recorder and played it back to them. They laughed and hugged each other in embarrassed delight, but the old man harangued and chastised the children and they lapsed into silence. "Now do it again, and do it properly" he must have said to them. He signalled to David to start recording and the children all sang seriously, accompanied by the twanging strings. The old man was satisfied as he listened to the replay. He raised his hand in salute and hobbled off down the road.

We had two ferry crossings during the day; the first a very ramshackle affair, merely boards slung across four metal canoes. Eight shining black bodies bent ready. Their paddles flashed in and out of the water with a regular plop and splash and we felt sure that at any moment they would break into a Paul Robeson chant.

The second one was much more sophisticated with an engine. A large plate screwed to the side said that it had been bought by U.S. aid. Hubert and Doris had caught up with us and edged their Volkswagen onto the platform behind us. The captain started the engine and we chugged off down the river through thick floating weed. As the engine slowed, the ferry drifted back upstream with the current towards the other bank. We missed the ramp completely. "You'd think this was the first time they'd ever done it" David exclaimed impatiently as we began the third attempt to dock and line up with the old planks which formed the ramp. Success at last.

"Go and watch the back of the vehicle" David instructed Peter, taking back two elastic bungees from one of the Africans who had just helped himself as we were watching the landing stage. The Land Rover drove off without any difficulty, but Susan and I watched with some misgivings as the trailer dipped and crashed up and down alarmingly.

"I wonder what broke open this time" she said, wringing her hands.

Hubert then drove his van down the ramp but stopped abruptly at the grinding sound of metal on the jagged stones. The van was almost standing on its nose in the sharp dip, its bumper caught on a huge boulder. After a quick bounce and heave by the men, though, the van shuddered and staggered up the slope.

We had decided to drive in convoy to the Catholic Mission at Binga. Twelve thousand acres of rubber and palm plantation spread out on either side. At first they looked unkempt and overgrown but as we drew nearer to Binga they were obviously thriving and well worked. We pointed out the little silver cups lashed to the rubber trees and speculated about the rows and rows of sturdy but not tall palm trees. Binga and the area around it had been part of an old Belgian plantation, but now it was the personal property of President Mobutu. The associated estate buildings were seedy and down at heel with sagging window frames.

After a few mistakes and wrong turnings we arrived at the Mission with its large church and well kept gardens. We found the night guardian, but not the Father, he was out visiting. It seemed presumptuous to unpack and settle in without asking permission, but the Father was not expected back until seven, well after dark, and we were all very hungry. We compromised by just unpacking food and cooking equipment and made supper in the twilight. "I can smell onions, fabulous!" said the Belgian priest as he puttered to a halt on his motor scooter. He turned out to be a charming man, and not at all perturbed by the band of dirty gypsies in front of his house. He welcomed us to the mission and offered us the use of two visitors' rooms plus showers and toilets. "I can sell you cold beer and cokes for the children" he told us, "come and join me for drinks about eight." "I'm the last of the Mohicans" he laughed, as we stretched out in the comfortable chairs on his veranda after a welcome shower. "There were three of us here, one was called back home, one drowned in the river two weeks ago and now I am alone. There are 50 million people in my parish." We so enjoyed our cheerful evening conversation with the priest, who hopped from English to French to German with ease and told us about the plantation and the people he cared for. He tried to persuade us to stay for a few days and really learn something about Africa. He was so right when he said that travellers like us tended to flash through the villages and countryside and gathered nothing but a superficial impression of the country—and often a misguided one. David felt we should push on. Susan and I had to agree.

The bell for early mass at 5.30 a.m. ended a hot sticky night. As we rolled down the gentle slope of the drive Sean shouted to David. "The trailer is making that noise again." It was the wheel bearings still causing trouble. Peter dragged out the tool box and they stripped, greased and reassembled the wheel in record time. "Damn" said David, scratching himself with his dirty hands when we were moving once more "I've been bitten to death for days. There must be more mosquitoes than we realize." His body was covered in groups of pink bumps and red and white lines where he had rubbed and scored his skin.

We finally reached the river Zaire at Lisala. The river boat for Kisangani had arrived and was due to leave later in the day. We felt it would be a terrific experience to travel upriver by boat for a couple of days, but we had one problem. As yet we had still not found anywhere to change currency. We enquired about prices and tickets and hunted round for a bank but found nothing. Undecided we sat down and did a few sums. It was going to be a very expensive trip to take the Land Rover and trailer on the river—it would cost about $100 more than driving. Too much, we agreed, and had another look at the map. We drove to Gemena, but there was no bank and no petrol. We checked our tanks and jerry cans. We had enough to get us to Bumba but then we would be stuck, we would need money then and fuel. Winding away from the river, we changed seats putting one of the children on waving duty in the passenger seat to give our aching arms a rest.

The Catholic mission at Bumba was rather elusive but we eventually found it and parked on the rough football pitch next to the boys' dormitories. The Abbe was a gentle African who seemed rather reluctant to let us stay. Previous groups of campers had left his showers and lavatories in a disgusting state and littered the grounds with their rubbish. Another Land Rover with four young occupants pulled up behind us. David asked the Abbe to come and meet our children and we assured him that we would treat his facilities with respect and request the other group to do the same.

We seemed to have lost Hubert and Doris. I rushed across round the side of the church in the darkness when I thought I heard their Volkswagen on the road but it was gone before I got there. On my way back to our camp I passed a group of the resident boys on their way to prep. "Bonsoir" I said quietly. "You're not French, are you?" asked one shyly in English. "No, we're English" I told him, "you speak very good English, did you learn it here?" A little group gathered round, all speaking with very little accent and excellent grammar. "Can we come across to your tent at 8.30 p.m. after prep and talk to you?" they requested. "Of course, we'll look forward to that."

I went back to help with the camp beds and mosquito nets. David came back from a short chat with the Abbe. We liked to try and leave something behind when we left. "If you have any spare tea girls, the Abbe would appreciate it for the boys; they haven't been able to buy any for weeks."

At 8.30 p.m. six visitors perched around on the camp beds, all about 16 years old. They were so sweet and chattered happily. "Would we send them some English books and sports magazines", they asked. One swopped names with Peter and asked him to write when we got back to England. The bell rang for lights out in the dormitories and they left reluctantly but promised to be back early in the morning before we left.

I approached the two English boys in the other Land Rover with whom we had already had long chats and swapped some fruit. I wondered if they had anything they could leave for the boys at the mission or make a small contribution for the church. They made me feel like a pious do-gooder. I returned to our camp completely deflated having been told they considered it totally unnecessary and even insulting to offer anything to the Abbe in return for his facilities and kindness. I felt very old next to these twenty year olds who seemed to think that life and Africa owed them something.

Quiet figures crept across the damp grass in the half light. One of the boys held out a piece of paper with 3 names and addresses on it, another asked Peter for his name and address so they could be pen pals. The Abbe smiled appreciatively at the large box of tea bags I pressed into his hand and he assured us the boys would enjoy breakfast for the next few days.

We drove round the small town but were thwarted in our early start. There only seemed to be one bank and it did not open until 8 am. We waited impatiently. David stood by the door as the bolts were drawn back but was stopped in his tracks when the cashier told him they did not have a licence to change foreign currency. We had to have money, we had no petrol. David dumped us on the bank of the river with the trailer and went off to scour the town. No sooner had he gone than a tall middle aged African dashed across waving his arms, shouting and pointing at us. We scrambled to our feet uncertainly as he continued to rant and rave. What had we done or not done? Susan and I looked at each other bewildered and then saw, both at the same moment, the badge pinned to his jacket "Sheriff" which was from a children's cowboy set. A smiling bystander tapped his forehead with his finger and then pointed at our abuser. We grinned, relaxed and saluted the 'Sheriff' as he ambled off calling down the wrath of heaven on everyone he saw.

David eventually found a little man in a grubby backyard office, his Mercedes parked outside. He changed our money, but at half the official rate. No wonder he could afford such an expensive car. We filled up our tanks and jerry cans, bought bread, bananas and pineapples from the little stalls on the outskirts of town.

The roads deteriorated alarmingly, becoming nothing more than a narrow potholed track with swamp on either side. Long sections had been repaired or reinforced with logs covered by dried grass. We crashed unsuspectingly into one hole after another. Many of the small bridges were rotten. We climbed out time and time again to straighten the planks, line up the wheels and search around for stronger looking logs to bear our weight. Turning one corner, an enormous chimpanzee lolloped across the road and disappeared into the dense jungle, curious large black and white birds flew high in the trees above us. We lost and re-found the river at varying intervals during the day. A beautiful, broad, lazy waterway with little floating islands of purple water lilies drifting gently downstream. Hoping to catch the ferry at Basoko, we ploughed on and despite the dreadful roads covered about 110 miles. The boat had gone when we arrived,

Susan and I were secretly relieved as David had been muttering about another all night drive and we did not feel up to it. "Oh well" he said, gazing out over the river, "Let's see if we can find some cold beer, and then the Catholic mission." "Ou se trouve du biere?" we called to one pedestrian after another. At last an obliging man climbed in next to the children and guided us through the winding lanes to the beer house—the bottles were not cold but we drank them just the same.

We camped on the banks of the river in the mission grounds and hoped the crocodiles and alligators would not find us. Thankfully, only the belching of the bull frogs and irritating buzz of the mosquitoes disturbed our peace. Anxious not to miss the first crossing, we arrived at the ferry at 6.30 and made breakfast while we waited. True to rumour, things started happening at about 8 a.m. Our notes on this section of the journey suggested an hour long crossing of the river so we all got out and stretched and yawned and prepared to sun ourselves. Ten minutes later the pilot made his first bid for the landing stage on the opposite bank. He made it in two. It seemed a very quick trip to the southern side of the river but who were we to argue.

The details in our books promised us reasonable dirt road so with any luck we would be in Kisangani before dark, although we would still have to cross backwards and forwards across the river twice more. The track went from bad to worse, huge potholes, deep mud and swamp sections that called for low ratio 4 wheel drive and left us shaking and apprehensive. We looked at our notes again, they described rubber plantations, but we could see nothing but dense encroaching jungle. The temperature was 100^0 and the humidity unbearable. We drank liberal quantities of fluid and wiped our red damp faces with cologne tissues. The compass sung wildly, it upset us that we seemed to travel south west for a lot of the time instead of south east. "Isangi?" shouted David to a small group of villagers. They pointed forward. That was the next ferry crossing. There seemed nothing for it but to carry on. "This track is about to disappear altogether" I said to Susan through closed teeth as I swung the wheel and shouted to the children to hold on tightly. We wallowed and lurched across a deep trench, the long grass brushing the sides of the Land Rover and low outstretched branches clouting the roof rack. Except for an occasional twinkle the thick interlaced trees and creepers blotted out the sun and linked hands across the sky above us. We swept round a bend and stopped with a lurch at the sight of a huge tree across the track. The boys ran forward to have a look and waved and shouted at me to plough through the vegetation to the right. We had to go, it was quite impossible to turn round and go back. At every little group of huts we shouted the same question "Isangi?" We got rather conflicting advice but the general consensus of opinion was straight on.

Susan took her turn at the wheel and had one of her 'lefting' days, when she barely gave anything or anyone on the left hand side of the vehicle room to breath or move and the passengers shrank away from the windows as another ugly branch loomed dangerously close. The marshy ground on either side was most disconcerting, it gave no room to manoeuver round big holes or obstructions, but Susan decided to try it and one wheel sank with a loud sucking noise and flicked up a muddy spray as it spun round and round. Poor Susan, sat with head in hands while the children groaned and moaned and declared us dead or gone for ever now, but they had not allowed for their Daddy's skill. We stood in a semicircle watching while David grunted and shunted swinging the wheel and changing gears at top speed, and finally urged the beast back onto firmer ground. He flung himself into the reclining seat with eyes closed, beads of perspiration sitting along his top lip. "Damn" he exploded, slapping his chest, "I've been bitten again." "Well it can't be mosquitoes, not during the day" I told him—"let's have a look." There were rows and collections of bites everywhere on his body. "Quick" I yelled, "something moved, there, catch it." He held out the squashed dead little black thing. "That's a flea" I said curling up my nose in disgust. "Isn't that a flea Susan? You have a look, your dog has always got fleas, you're always picking them off him." "Here's another one" said David holding out his hand. "Go away Daddy, we don't want your fleas" pleaded the children, clambering over the seats and cringing in the back of the Land Rover. "We don't want them either" laughed Susan and I together "You'd better get out and walk." David peeled off all his clothes except for a mini pair of underpants and we started the big flea hunt. We were horrified by the number we found. He was a walking flea circus. Where on earth had he caught them? We worked back over the days. "I can't remember when I first started to get bitten" he said, then after a few moments thought—"That night in Cameroun when we stayed in that strange little club." We laid the blame at the Frenchman's door, but we will never ever know where they came from. Perhaps most ridiculous of all, we had omitted to pack D.D.T. in our extensive medical kit. David reckoned the sheepskin cover on the seat was also alive with the little monsters so we gave it and him a wide birth for the rest of the day.

"There's the river" called Sarah, pointing out to the right. We all cheered, we must be on the right road after all. "Just a minute" said Susan, "what's the river doing on our right, it should be on our left. We are supposed to have been travelling for 100 miles along the south side of the Zaire after we crossed on the ferry." We felt completely disoriented. But just then the track swung round and joined a much better road. "Isangi?" shouted David to a group of villagers, stretched out in front of their huts. They pointed forward over the river. "I don't understand this" muttered David as we drove along beside the river, "let's have a look at the map again." Susan was always chief navigator, she put on her glasses and peered at all the lines and roads twisting round the Zaire. "I know what we've done" she slapped the map and held it out for us to see. "when we took the ferry this morning we didn't cross the Zaire. All we did was to nip across this little tributary leading into it and stayed on the north side of the river. We have been driving along the wrong side of it all day where there is no road marked at all, but we have made it and now we are at the point where the ferry brings you back across the river from Isangi. That's why all the Africans kept pointing forward—they just didn't think to tell us it was across the river." We were shattered, no wonder it had been such a ghastly road—well path really, not a road most of the time, but no harm was done, we were back to reasonable conditions again and would still reach Kisangani, though somewhat later than we had expected.

Everyone was tired and exhausted by the tension and unpleasant temperatures of the day. We stopped to buy bananas in a little village, they wanted cigarettes in exchange and one mimed a syringe going into his arm. We shook our heads and looked disapproving. David took over the wheel as darkness fell, only 20 miles to go! He wound up the Land Rover to a steady 40 m.p.h. and we watched the milometer click round rhythmically. He swung round a corner and the whole vehicle suddenly picked up speed as we hurtled down a steep slope, the headlights reflecting nothing but the bright white circles of themselves in the river below. He slammed on the brakes and the wheels locked as we continued to approach the water at an alarming rate, pushed from behind by our ton and a half of un-braked trailer. We shuddered to a halt only feet from the river, everything suddenly silent after the screams and scraping of the tyres. "Great stuff, fantastic" yelled Sean. "What a piece of driving" applauded Peter. "I think I'm going to be sick" said Susan disappearing into the shadows. "What's going on" asked Sarah totally unaware of the near disaster. David and I kept quiet. There was nothing really to say, except that the worst had not happened. We inspected the slope that had so nearly plunged us into the deep murky water. In our tiredness we had forgotten that there was one more ferry to cross before reaching Kisangani. We saw a dim light on the opposite back and flashed our headlights, the light flashed off and on in answer. We sat down to steady our racing hearts and shaking legs whilst the children continued to enthral about this latest bit of excitement.

As the ferry took us across the dark silent river, David told the Africans what had happened. They laughed; "You shouldn't drive so quickly" they told him. On arriving at the other side, David asked a passer by on the dark sidewalk in Kisangani. "Where's a good hotel?" "Zaire Palace" he replied "just up to the top of the road and round to the left." Lit by hundreds of lights on in every room and what with the large dining room on the second floor, it looked very 'posh'. We were filthy, Susan and I hung back not wanting to show ourselves in the bright foyer. The children returned in a few minutes followed by a porter. Sean climbed on Peter's shoulders and began untying the roof rack cover. "If we run and keep our heads down no-one will see us" I told Susan. "I'm too tired to go any further, we have to stay here." "What about my fleas?" David asked me, viewing the double bed, the first we had seen since leaving England. I had temporarily forgotten about his little friends. "Have a soak in a bath, then have a shower and then wash all over in antiseptic solution. We'll share the little devils that are left."

CHAPTER 10

PIGMIES AND HIPPOS . . .

"IN SICKNESS AND in health" I chanted, flicking a dead flea off the sheets and heading for the shower with a bottle of antiseptic. "What's the programme today?" David looked down into the little courtyard with its high wall and heavy padlocked gates where he had parked our Land Rover and trailer the evening before. "We've got quite a few problems on the vehicle" he told me, "Last night when I was parking it, the gear box momentarily refused to engage any gear and I need a couple of welding jobs done on it as well. I'm hoping some of those likely looking lads down there will help me to clean it inside and out. We can't go on in this state of filth and dust."

It sounded like a busy day. After a slow relaxed breakfast, I unpacked my airmail pad to catch up on a few letters—was it really the 22nd January? It seemed a lifetime since we had left home and the Sahara was already becoming part of a dream. Every day conditions and problems changed but we had been very lucky so far, nothing had occurred to cause a major hitch in our expedition and we were all very fit and well and revelling in our new experiences. The children had been amazing, adapting daily to their strange routine and maturing visibly with their added responsibilities and team work. I hoped we would continue to be as happy and fortunate.

Somewhere along the line the clocks had changed again, our watches were all an hour wrong, accounting for the impatient glances of the waiters and empty dining room. It proved to be quite a comic hotel, and not the mini-Hilton it had looked like through tired eyes the night before. At one time it had obviously been a thriving establishment, equipped with expensive modern gadgets, but as things had broken down or worn out they had just been left. None of the lifts worked and similarly most of the air conditioners merely remained as museum pieces. Large ragged holes gaped in the carpets; there were no handles on the bathroom doors and to my disgust no seat on the loo. I had been looking forward to sitting in comfort instead of squatting, jeans clutched in one hand.

Susan went off to look for the post office as usual; I did feel she should have left a scribble on each post office wall marking her trail across Africa. We teased her continually about her obsession, but her mother was delighted to get regular news of our progress and safety. She came back sweating profusely and described the ghostly remains of a once busy town. There seemed little to buy and less to eat—a bit of dried fish and bread seemed the only things available, or perhaps the only things the local mums could afford to buy; as usual prices were ridiculous.

David found 'a man', like he always managed to find 'a man' wherever we went. This one was a real find, a British Leyland representative who arranged for our trailer to be welded free of charge but he could not help us track down any wheel bearings. The gear box seemed to have righted itself, at least for the time being after a night's rest, so the only thing that remained was a thorough hosing and clean out. Two of the hotel staff helped to strip off and scrub the seat covers, especially the one we suspected of harbouring more fleas. They then, with David's help and instructions, took out all the loose equipment and floor mats and washed and scraped at the thick layer of red dust which had crept under every crevice and along every ledge. Streams of murky water poured across the yard and trickled out of the gate into the gutter as our Land Rover was slowly transformed back to its smart sweet smelling self. They rubbed and polished until it gleamed while David did a comprehensive engine service and changed the oil—the filter contained an inch of dirt and grit! It was a formidable task for him in the intolerable humidity and temperature but he battled on, determined we should be in good order for the next rough section ahead.

I watched most of the proceedings from my air conditioned bedroom—I only left it that day when a rumbling tummy insisted it was time to eat. I made the most of the quiet day and sat the children down to some school work. They had escaped fairly lightly so far and apart from oral quizzes and mental arithmetic they had done next to nothing. We skipped lunch as the food was terribly expensive, though I must confess excellent, and much as we would like to have waded through the menu we were by this stage paying almost $1 per gallon for petrol and had to keep our priorities right.

We waited impatiently for David in the hotel room longing to go down to dinner. He burst into the room, slammed the door and leant against it laughing. "What's so funny?" I asked him when he stopped puffing. "I was just affecting an escape" he explained "two young ladies downstairs decided tonight was my night and they have been following me all over the hotel. I've just managed to lose them by leading them up to the top floor and then doing a quick double back down the service stairway. I didn't want them to find out our room number." "I can see Susan and I had better escort you to the bar before supper" I told him "that should put them off." "I'll say" he laughed, "the Africans in the yard this afternoon were congratulating me on having two such big strong looking wives, I didn't bother to tell them that Susan and I are just good friends." David had plans for another all night drive from Kisangani to Oicha in Western Zaire. We were well rested and had caught up with our washing and servicing.

"I wonder what we'll find missing this morning" David grunted, rolling over and looking at his watch as I cuddled down for another 10 minutes at dawn. Theoretically our gear should have been very safe in the walled, locked courtyard with two all night guardians. Eventually I stretched and yawned and tottered over to draw back the curtains. I looked down into the yard at the Land Rover. It did not look quite right, but for a moment I could not think why. "Oh no" I groaned "all our polythene water carriers have gone off the roof rack" David leapt out of bed and joined me at the window. "Bastards. I bet I know who did that, one of the so-called helpers kept asking me for them yesterday." He dragged his clothes on quickly, buttoning his shirt as he hurried off downstairs.

Five minutes later an almighty row started out in the courtyard and went on for about three quarters' of an hour. Everyone shouted and pointed and became more and more excited and as the Manager came on the scene, wild accusations filled the air. Even the small polythene container for the cooker petrol had gone. According to the guardians they had grown feet and walked away themselves in the night. They could offer no other explanation. David was very, very angry, white faced and grim he followed the Manager back to his office. "I intend to report this to the police" he told him, drumming his fingers on the desk. The Manager was full of apologies and obviously quite worried. "We've had a lot of problems with the police" he told David "surely we can work this out" David scowled silently. "Do you want a full receipt for your bill?" asked the Manager. David shrugged his shoulders. The manager quickly jotted down a few figures. He charged us for only one night instead of two and for no food at all. We totted it up as we drove out of Kisangani later in the morning; he had undercharged us by about $80!

All set for another 36 hour marathon, we settled into our driving routine again, stopping each hour to change seats, make odd snacks and plan our programme. We had done about 120 miles when Peter called to David from the back of the Land Rover. "Daddy, the trailer seems to be riding very low, at a strange angle." David glanced in the driving mirror, did not like what he saw and pulled into the edge of the road. We all climbed out and crowded round the back. One of the bolts on the trailer hitch had sheared off completely; it was held only by the second one and was shaking and dipping wildly. We did not have another bolt and there was no garage sign on the map for at least another hundred miles. Susan and I looked at each other in despair. David climbed up on to the roof rack and threw down of all things a stainless steel boat shroud. Together we tied it round the trailer arm and to the Land Rover to take the strain off the remaining bolt and limped on slowly along the road. After 3 or 4 miles we saw a lorry parked haphazardly on the other side of the road. Two figures were toiling up the hill ahead of us carrying a battery. We stopped as we drew alongside the sweating breathless pair, moved our bits into a corner and made room for them. "Are you taking that to a garage?"

David asked them, nodding at their battery. They shook their heads. "Back to our boss man, he give us another." They grinned at the children.

"Do you know if there is a garage nearby?" David asked. They chattered and mumbled together in low voices. "Perhaps at the next village, Bafwasende." one of them replied. We dropped them at the top of the hill and they plodded off through the undergrowth along a narrow track, stopping every few minutes to stretch out on the grass and take a breather. Bafwasende was about 40 miles away, so we drove slowly and carefully with one eye on the trailer the whole way. As the first huts of the village appeared, we slowed down to a walking pace looking hopefully for anything that resembled a garage. A local shop owner waved and held up bottles of orange—not what we wanted, but he might know where to go. David nipped out and had a word with him. He pulled on a jacket and ran alongside us up the road shouting instructions. Finally we stopped and David followed him between the mud huts. We all sat silently in the Land Rover, the heat and humidity draining us of energy and enthusiasm. We smiled weakly at the group of children who gathered round to inspect us. They did not seem to notice the oppressive atmosphere. Just when I thought I could not sit there for one more minute, David returned, closely followed by an African in a boiler suit who climbed in next to me. "This man is a mechanic" said David, "He's going to try and help me, but first he's going to take us to the Roman Catholic Mission so that I can leave you all there with the trailer."

We eventually found a short round African Father in the scrappy outbuildings next to the tiny church. He welcomed us to camp on the patch of grass next to the church and David unloaded all the gear off the top of the roof rack and unhitched the trailer before heading back to the village clutching half a loaf of bread and a pineapple. Susan and I looked at the pile of equipment on the grass and groaned. We did not feel like doing anything, it was so hot and steamy, but the light was already failing and it was always easier to cope before dark. There was no loo and no water, which was bad news, and by then we were reduced to two small polythene containers which always travelled inside the Land Rover after losing all our others. One of these was empty and the other only two thirds full. The Father had gone off down the road in his rattling old car so we had to make do.

We decided we must put up the tent because the dew was so heavy and soaked everything in a matter of minutes. We cursed and swore at the frame unable to find one of the cross pieces and finally dragged the canvas over without it and hoped it would not collapse. We cooked in the light from the battery and saved a large helping for David as I knew he would be starving by the time he got back!

Within minutes of touching the pillow, three tired children were fast asleep. Susan and I sat drinking coffee in the darkness, waiting. It was 9 p.m. when we saw the Land Rover's headlamps coming up the hill and swing round across the ditch to the side of the tent. David staggered out, filthy and exhausted. He and the mechanic had spent three hours on their backs taking out the petrol tank so that they could reach the wretched bolts on the hitch. David cursed this piece of design on the Land Rover. The little garage did not have another bolt, but as luck would have it, a government Land Rover standing nearby awaiting repairs had a similar tow hitch. The proprietor of the garage offered David one of the bolts off it for $12—we had to have it, so we had to pay.

Determined not to be done out of his all night run, David had us all up at 3 a.m. Packing in the dark was always difficult and dangerous. We tripped over tent pegs and fell into two large holes in the flattened grass between the tent and the vehicle. More than once we dropped armfuls of equipment as we stumbled around, still tired and reluctant to move on so early. Before creeping quietly away we left some tins of dried milk and butter on the Father's doorstep. The mission appeared to be very poor compared with some of the ones we had previously stayed at.

We climbed steadily all day into the rain forests. The vegetation was different in character from the jungle near the Zaire river. The trees were shorter with fewer struggling creepers, although extremely lush. We saw fewer birds and butterflies and strangely enough the humidity seemed lower. The rain forest was well named, as we ran into a tropical downpour in the middle of the morning. The water ran down the hillsides in rivulets carving muddy channels and splashing, in long reddish streaks, along the side of the Land Rover. The broad green leaves bowed on their succulent stalks as the rain drops drummed on their glossy smooth surface, only to spring like divers and land on some other plant below. "I just have to go to the toilet" said Sean. "Not in this darling, surely, can't you wait" I asked. "Nope" he replied simply. He returned to the Land Rover five minutes later with hair plastered over his ears, his shirt transparent and his trousers clinging round his legs. "You should stand out there" he gasped breathlessly. "It feels absolutely fantastic." It looked tempting but we didn't try it.

We were almost at one of the most dreaded stretches of the whole trip. Other overlanders had previously told us that it could take three days to cover just 16 miles in the most appalling road conditions imaginable. We were not looking forward to getting our trailer through that lot. But as the miles rolled by we saw a lot of evidence of road works and piles of fresh earth at the side of the track. The Beni mud holes no longer existed, the grader had recently been along and skimmed a beautiful new surface for us.

The stature and features of many of our silent watchers was distinctly different. We had reached Pygmy country and although most of Pygmies prefer to remain deep in the forest, some had moved to the roadside and had built little collections of leafy huts which blended with the backcloth.

"Puncture, puncture" yelled Peter suddenly. It was the same nearside trailer wheel. We quickly had an inquisitive audience to watch our strange performance of changing a wheel. One old man stood puffing on a strange curly pipe, made of a piece of bent aluminium off a car. He pointed at the funny little bowl and held out his hand. I fished out a cigarette and gave it to him thinking he would open it up and take out the tobacco, but he simply stuck it into the bowl, lit it and went off happily puffing at his chimney. Then, of course, they all wanted a cigarette!

By 5 p.m. we reached our planned destination of Oicha and located the American Protestant Mission. It was a large spreading complex of bungalows and gardens and fairly large hospital units with a leper colony on the outskirts. One small grassy area was set aside for campers and was complete with all facilities and an open sided hut, big enough for sleeping in and dining on a large table lined by wooden benches. We were filthy and tired and longed for bed. "Watch out for petty thieving" the Americans at the Mission had warned us, so we set the alarm in the Land Rover and stretched a long string from the front bumper to the camping shelter. Having tied a light aluminium chair to the end of the string, we propped it up on the wall. "That will be our early warning device," David assured us as we tucked the mosquito nets under our sleeping bags. In a matter of seconds he was snoring loudly. I tossed fitfully for a while, listening to the sudden storm and teeming rain before drifting off into welcome oblivion. A sudden crash startled me into trembling wakefulness. Propped on one elbow I peered into the darkness, but the only sound was the patter of the rain on the tin roof, and the snorts and grunts from my sleeping family. "There's something out there" I whispered hoarsely to David, but he ground his teeth and turned over. I fumbled for the torch under my pillow and struggled to disentangle my mosquito net and find my boots before groping my way over to the doorway. The aluminium chair lay in a heap on the ground. Something or someone had tripped across the line. My mouth felt dry and my heart was racing, but I decided that the intruder was probably as frightened as I was so I boldly flashed my torch into the pitch black night. A hand tore down the inside of my belly as eyes reflected in the torchlight and a nearby bush rustled and crackled and then went quiet. I waited, switching off my torch and listening to my own raid breathing in the stillness. Nothing moved, our visitor seemed to have gone. I picked up the chair and re-fixed the booby-trap as before and after a complete check round the camp climbed back into bed but sleep was slow to come and when it did, only for short snatched periods. I checked our camp repeatedly into the early grey dawn before I finally lapsed into a deep dreamless sleep.

The children woke us with cups of steaming hot coffee—in bed as a special treat. We stretched and lounged while I teased everyone about all the wild animals I had had to fend off in the night to ensure their good night's sleep, but no-one believed me. Susan and I viewed the trailer with disgust. The red dust of the roads had collected in piles over everything. Inside our large plastic boxes damaged tins of evaporated milk had swollen and exploded, showering their sour contents over the other food, and filtering through the cracks to ooze and spread round the loose equipment. We began the long unpack and scraping of the foul smelling dirt and the inevitable washing and repacking of all the tins. The worst damage always occurred in the back third of the trailer as it seemed to do a double catapult gyration over the bumps and holes in the track. There seemed no way to beat the continual destruction of our supplies as the driving conditions continued to deteriorate. Fortunately, we were very well stocked and had more than enough for our personal needs, but the wastage of good food distressed us deeply, particularly driving through country where a large percentage of the population were so hungry and underfed.

We all wanted to visit a Pygmy village before we moved on. David located the chief of the area who instructed him to return with us all after lunch and we would be accompanied by his men. It was all highly organised and slightly forbidding. When we rolled up in the afternoon, three guides were waiting for us, two crammed into the Land Rover and one hung onto the ladder at the back. The boss man was a tall wiry important young man clad in red shirt and high black boots. He directed the operation with great authority and plenty of displays of temper. At his direction we wound our way along a very bumpy track, a mere footpath through the jungle with huge holes and patches of marsh for about 4 miles before we finally arrived at the selected village. Most of the menfolk were out hunting, we were told, as we parked at the perimeter and walked among the collection of haphazardly arranged shanty-like, igloo shaped huts made out of dried palm leaves.

We stood in a silent group while our guides harangued the Pygmy women and children and elderly men into a disorganised chant and made them shuffle round in a circular dance. Misinterpreting our pained expressions at this humiliating performance, our guide then bent low and disappeared into the huts, dragging out more screaming children and reluctant mothers and made them perform for us, pushing and nudging them if they attempted to break the line or stop singing. Photography was forbidden, but David taped their not very melodious drumming on hollow logs and played it back to them to their delight.

The chief guide then drove a stake into the ground and the men and boys demonstrated their skill with the bows and arrows. The day was stolen by a tiny tot barely big enough to hold the bow, but who scored a direct hit first shot. We cheered and clapped and his mother proudly paraded him, just like I do at sports day, when one of my offspring comes in first. Suddenly the negotiations started. The chief guide told us we must pay the Pygmies for their hospitality. "How much do you think?" asked David. The three men went into a huddle and then called David over. He shrugged and handed me a bundle of notes—it was the equivalent of $5. "See if you can give this to the chief's wife" he told me, a charming old lady. I felt rather nervous as everyone was watching especially the officious guides. I stuffed the money into my bag and got out sweets, matches and biros and gave them to the children, hoping to divert attention but when I tried quietly to give the money to the Pygmies, I found a watcher at my shoulder. We could not beat the system. Anyway, I dug into my make-up purse and gave the young mums a mirror and a collection of half-used lipsticks and eye shadows as we climbed back into the Land Rover and waved goodbye. We were all rather silent and saddened by our circus like experience, but held our tongues as we still had company. On the way back further negotiations started. "Do you realise that your guides should receive a gift?" asked one of the Africans. We nodded and handed him a peppermint. "Money is acceptable" he added. We looked at each other in silence and offered them a cigarette. When we arrived back at their headquarters, it cost David a further $6 before they broke into smiles then handshakes all round.

Driving back into the area of the hospital, Susan and I stopped off to look around. We located an American nurse, who had been working there for over 20 years. I cannot even remember her name but she was one of those wonderful people you meet as you storm through life, who is dedicated to the service of others and who carries with them a much longed-for tranquillity and love of mankind which makes you feel the richer for having met them. She took us on a full tour of the hospital and leper colony and answered all our questions patiently and serenely as we marvelled and expressed our admiration at the work undertaken. The Pygmy babies were beautiful—only 3-4 lbs. in weight but needing no special incubation or care. They fed hungrily from their beaming mothers, while the fathers fed the mother rice soup which they brought in from their villages. The facilities were very basic and run on typical African lines. The families fed and nursed their relatives within the hospital accommodation. Rows and rows of tiny houses lined the grounds where patients lived, presenting themselves each day for outpatient treatment. A qualified doctor visited the hospital once a month. Emergencies, surgical or otherwise, were looked after by a male nurse. Similarly the dentist, in his own little office complete with X-ray equipment, still short of spare parts, was self trained, but I gathered highly efficient. Any important pathological investigations were sent to England—results took at least two months. Likewise drugs came by boat from England and were often long awaited. Susan and I felt we saw real medicine as it is practiced without the sophisticated equipment and machinery that we have grown to expect in our affluent society.

Oxen grazed lazily in the grounds, driven there by their proud owners to escape the tsetse fly, the source of sleeping sickness. Flocks of goats munched everything in sight. "Surely with all these oxen and goats, the population must have a fairly high protein intake?" we asked the nurse. She shook her head smiling at our lack of appreciation of African life.

"The oxen are beasts of labour" she told us "and the goats are valuable as dowries, but of course they provide milk which helps." We felt rather insular and ignorant, but our horizons had been considerably widened by meeting and talking to these wonderful people. When we re-joined the family, Peter and Sean were having a tremendous game of football with the local children. The African boys were great, they ran my two into the ground. David announced his intention for another all night drive. He seemed to think that a two night stopover would reinforce our energies, Susan and I rolled our eyes and sighed. We packed as much as possible before bedding down, to make for an easy early start next day. We had been joined at the camping site by a strange young American couple who sat cross-legged on the table to eat their meals, which left us feeling first; middle-aged and square, and then slightly outraged at this seemingly antisocial behaviour. As an established family following the so-called hippie trail across Africa, we often felt slightly at odds with the antics, dress and general behaviour of some of the younger generation.

Moving on from Oicha we had a delightful day on hard, but rough-fissured roads, climbing up into the Ruwensori Mountains—the mountains of the moon, a gloriously romantic sounding name. The scenery was stunning in cool non-humid air, the roads bending and twisting forever upwards. We reached 7,500ft on these rough roads, up through the mountains covered with trees and steep un-terraced fields of sweet corn and bananas. Scarlet blossoms decorated the forest and huge fernlike bracken trees and evergreens with flat Japanese shapes floated like parasols on the ends of delicate branches. Around every bend we saw new greenery. Green views in the foreground, and distant blue mountains, remote and beyond our reach.

There was nowhere to pull off the road but we found a slight niche under some Eucalyptus trees at about 5 pm and stopped to cook a large meal. I pushed the boat out and made croutons for the soup, followed by bacon and eggs with tomatoes. We had parked near a little footpath that wound up the hill beside the road. As we squatted on the bank eating our supper, a local family who obviously lived at the top of the hill, quietly collected to watch us. We felt slightly embarrassed about having parked at their front gate and blocking their way and apologised as best we could. As we packed up all our bits and pieces, we gave them biros and a very large box of matches. The father let out a spontaneous whoop of delight and broke into a rousing song and dance routine, accompanied by a twangy finger instrument played by his friend. We handed round cigarettes and parted with great goodwill, both sides clapping the other.

It was already dark as we left, but there was a full moon and we could see the pale bleached slopes of the hills against the night sky which lit up spasmodically with great flashes of lightning way over on the right. The children curled up in the back on their foam mattresses, intertwining their legs and arms until they found a comfortable spot and we started our hourly routine of sleep, co-driving and driving. At about 9 p.m. we reached the gate leading into the game reserve. There was a large notice at the side of it. "Closed between 6 p.m. and 6 a.m." I read aloud. "That seems to be the end of our all night drive." The gate keeper appeared and closing his hand round the money David offered, opened the gate without any questions and waved us through. We were delighted, perhaps now we would see some African wildlife as it roamed by night. There were plenty of optimistic road signs denoting elephants and our hopes soared even further but we did not see one. Water buffalo and deer were the best we could do until suddenly a large hippopotamus lumbered onto the road and stood staring dourly into our headlights. "Wake up, wake up" I yelled at the children in a great state of excitement and shaking them roughly. "Oh Sean, do wake up and look." We subsequently saw lots more hippos big and small grazing among the bushes and every now and again two bright eyes would appear and watch us pass, but it was impossible to

identify their owner in the darkness. In the middle of the park there
was a lodge camp with accommodation and guarded gates. We felt
sure they would put a stop to a night tour. No lights showed as we
approached but a barrier stretched across the road. David tiptoed over
to the night guard's hut and found him fast asleep as was their wont.
He quietly swung back the barrier and beckoned us through. The
Land Rover engine seemed to roar in the stillness and we felt sure
that at any moment a voice would challenge us and call us back, but
no-one stirred. In the distance we could see the glow from an active
volcano. Sean was absolutely fascinated by it and stayed awake for over
an hour just to look at it. The road continued through savannah type
country and then changed to large areas of swamp with the rising
steam from hot sulphurous springs, and again lots of hippopotami.

About 2 a.m. we arrived at the gate out of the reserve. This looked
very much more official with a padlocked barrier and the way round
blocked by broad concrete posts. At the other side an army lorry
was parked, empty but ominous. We could see no-one. We sat with
bated breath while David scouted round looking for a way out. Susan
was horrified and had visions of instant jail, covering her face with
her hands when David closely inspected the padlock and eventually
managed to slip it and raise the barrier. "Come on Susie, stop getting
in a state and drive through" I chivvied "Shush, don't rev the engine,
someone will hear us." She barely slowed down to let David jump
aboard as we left the park, sure we would be caught, but on we went.

Fatigue began to set in, as it always did at about 2-3 a.m. in the
morning. With heavy heads and aching eyes we peered ahead and saw
a lorry parked on the side of the road. Three Africans staggered across
the road as we drew level, they had two punctures but no tools. They
wanted to borrow our pump. The children woke up as the movement
of the Land Rover stopped and climbed out to go to the loo, Susan
and I dozed fitfully for half an hour while David supervised their
repairs. I felt rather cross at having to stop, I thought they should carry
their own tools on such poor deserted roads and not expect travellers
like ourselves to provide an R.A.C. service in the middle of the night.
We eventually got under way again but Susan had had enough, she
fell into a deep sleep and David and I shared the driving.

"I don't feel very well" Sarah suddenly announced from the hot
heavy breathing group in the back. She clambered over the sleeping

figures onto my knee and I opened the window to give her some air. "I'm going to be sick." David stopped abruptly and I flung open the door. All the bumping up and down in the back had not agreed with her big fried supper and usually hardy stomach. I lifted her back onto my knee, pale but already feeling better at having got rid of the offending meal.

With only a few miles left to reach the border at Goma we stopped at 5 a.m. in the early dawn. We felt dirty, tired and scratchy, but as usual the children woke up in great spirits. We made coffee and cereals and Susan and I sat wearily in the Land Rover with our mugs, irritated by the incessant chatter of the children, while David, much to our astonishment, climbed up onto the roof rack and promptly fell asleep for an hour.

"I've lost my boots" wailed Sarah. "You're just not looking" I told her crossly. Peter rummaged around among the foam and sleeping bags.

"They're not here Sarah." With an impatient growl I climbed into the back to look but could not see them. "You must have kicked them out when you all got up to go to the loo. That really is too bad, now all you have got are your sandals", I stormed. The children surveyed me in silence; I was too tired to be reasonable.

David felt refreshed after his cat-nap, but I could not stay awake another minute and fell soundly asleep, jaw slack, knees curled up in the foetal position on the reclining seat. I woke up two hours later to find us parked in a garage in Goma. David had already had our punctured tyre fixed using his own tools and repair patches and they had found a coffee shop for breakfast and bread. My mouth was dry and tasted foul, my neck was stiff and I had pins and needles in one foot. I needed 2 large cups of coffee before I could face the day.

Walking down the main street, we stopped to look round the tourist shops, all selling ivory and wood carvings, but the quality was poor and the prices ridiculous as always. We still had some Zairen currency left but decided to use it for petrol, but unfortunately the pumps were dry.

"How much local money have you got?" asked the customs man as we presented ourselves at the border. "Very little" answered David. He had told me to hide the bulk of it. "You are not allowed to take it with you" he said, holding out his hand. We were glad we had not declared it all as he stuffed it into his pocket and stamped our passports. It was a great system, but all one way. For the first time customs and police were in the same office, it was such a relief and saved a lot of time and aggravation having to do things and answer questions only once instead of twice as had occurred so far.

As we moved down the road to the Rwandan customs and police post, we looked back at the smoky volcano behind Goma, feeling pleased to have crossed so many rugged miles without mishap, but a little sad that we were about to embark on the last section of our journey.

CHAPTER 11

SO MANY FRONTIERS AND SO MANY FORMS . . .

"CAMPING IS NOT allowed" scowled the Rwandan policeman, tapping our forms with his pen. "You must stay in hotels." We nodded obediently and corrected the eighteen forms we had just completed before joining the short queue once more. "You must buy visas" he said, still not prepared to flourish the rubber stamp we had now grown so accustomed to. "Can you change us some money?" asked David. "No, it's not allowed, you must change it in a bank." "Will you accept French francs or sterling for the visas?" pressed David. "No" he replied firmly "but I will take American dollars." We shook our heads and walked away to have a conference. We had reached an impasse. "Now what?" I asked David, "If we can't get into the country, we can't go to a bank and if we don't go to a bank we can't get it—this is quite ridiculous."

David collected the handful of forms from us "Let's try again" he said and we followed him back to the office again. "What about Zaires?" he asked "will you accept them?" Susan and I promptly turned on our heels and walked quickly back to the Land Rover. We were not supposed to have any Zaires having just left the country and we could see the Zaire Police strolling about only a few yards up the road. David followed five minutes later, obviously cross. "They all want their cut" he muttered "that cost me $10."

If we couldn't camp we would either have to stay in the border town or drive on to the capital Kigali or find a hotel. As it was only 10.30 a.m. David was all for driving on. Susan and I felt exhausted. "It's a good road" he encouraged us "tar seal most of the way, the man at the garage in Goma told me." We fell for it and agreed to drive on.

Rwanda was the most unexpectedly beautiful country to find in the heart of Africa. Land of a thousand hills and we climbed up and down every one of them on dreadful hard, bumpy, stony roads; hell for both the vehicle and drivers. The promised tar seal remained a far off dream and never materialized. We drove up the steep winding tracks labouring with our heavy load and marvelling as each bend revealed another exquisite view and higher peaks with sheer drops on either side of us. Every inch of every mountain side seemed to be cultivated, some terraced, but many too steep to terrace and the small bumpy fields just hung perpendicularly on their sides. There were people everywhere, working, hoeing, picking and for a change the men were working alongside their women folk as well. Grove after grove of banana trees filled the valleys and golden and green fields of sweet corn stretched as far as the eye could see. The cool clear air filled our lungs and the scent from the eucalyptus and mimosa tree wafted through our open windows. Many of the villagers smiled and waved but kept their distance and the children ran off into the fields as we approached and peeped shyly through the long grass.

We toiled on making slow progress and more than once we ran out of power as the Land Rover shuddered and groaned up the slopes and we had to engage low ratio to top the rise. This section of our journey was taking a terrible toll on our vehicle; the combination of continued steep climbs or descents on terrible road surface was likely to prove too much. Quite suddenly in the middle of the afternoon, the gearbox refused to engage any gear. Fortunately we were on a fairly flat stretch of road and could stop with safety. David scrambled underneath with a tin of oil and topped up the gear boxes and away we went, but ten minutes later when I tried to change into 2nd gear, it refused. "Don't force it, don't be heavy handed" instructed David as I waggled the lever. We ground to a halt and he climbed into the driving seat. He found that by pausing and going into reverse before each gear change he could keep us moving. It was obviously in a lot of trouble.

Susan spread out the map and measured the distance to Kigali. "It's 50 miles" she announced after a few minutes "and there's no town at all on the way." David drove the whole stretch nursing the sick truck and we reached the capital after dark, very thankful to have made it. "Where can I find a hotel?" shouted David to a petrol pump attendant. We followed his instructions but barely paused when the enormous luxurious and very expensive looking building came into view. We searched in vain for somewhere less ostentatious and more suitable to our purse. The answer was always the same, no rooms. I headed off on foot to make a few enquiries in a very noisy beer house and returned ten minutes later to find two African girls sitting in the Land Rover chatting to the children. They wanted a lift back to their hotel and assured us there were plenty of vacant rooms. We booked in without even bothering to inspect the accommodation, we had been driving for 36 hours and could not go one step further.

After a quick lick and a promise to hands and face we made for the dining room in search of a hot meal. The prices were extortionate—the cheapest meal being $3. We ordered and sat wearily in a silent group. "That's quite revolting" announced David pushing away his plate of curried chicken. There was nothing but a piece of bone and a thick floury mess laced with curry powder. Susan tackled hers unenthusiastically but she ate it, she never left any food. Fortunately, I had ordered veal for the rest of us and it was not too bad. "Give this back to the chef with my compliments" David told the waiter holding out his plate "it's never seen a chicken." The waiter threw back his head and roared with laughter as he carried it back to the kitchen. No alternative meal was produced. I was furious as David was tired and hungry. When they produced the bill half an hour later he refused to pay for his meal and only then did the Manager suggest he should choose another meal—but it was too late, for David needed sleep.

A tiny trickle of water spluttered out of the cold tap next morning, and nothing but a rude noise from the hot. Bathing in two inches of cold water was very unsatisfactory and unpleasant. But breakfast made up for it. We ate fresh pawpaw and cereals followed by omelettes and rolls. I warned the children to eat everything in sight as we would not be buying them lunch. A few crumbs on the table cloth were the only signs that we had been there as we all fled out of the dining room.

David had to sort out the gear box problem which sounded fairly major. Susan and I had the same old problem of dirty clothes and dirty people. Driving round the town David found a Land Rover centre with a very helpful Belgian mechanic. Listening to the symphonics he diagnosed our gear box problem and suggested a solution. The rubber sleeve on the lower end of the gear lever had broken up where it entered the selectors, a common problem on Series 3 Land Rovers. He could repair it quite easily by machining the corners off a nut and welding it to the lever, but as he explained, it would be very expensive if his workers had to do all the work. Peter and David brought the Land Rover back to the hotel and we all set too and removed all our bits and pieces and luggage. Then the two of them took the gearbox to pieces so that David could walk through the garage gates with only the parts needing repair—even so I think it must have been a solid gold nut that they welded onto our gear lever. Meanwhile back at the hotel Sean and Sarah did some long overdue school work and played with their few toys. At lunch time I fed them secretly in our room on cereals and bananas appointing one to act as look out for approaching hotel staff.

When David and Peter returned late in the afternoon, it was with a well running vehicle once more and they had even found a man to put a few stitches in the canvas covering of the aluminium chairs which had chaffed through by constant rubbing and vibration in the trailer. We had a family conference about supper. The prices were so ridiculous and the food so dreadful. We decided to bring in food and the petrol cooker from the trailer and make supper in our room. All set and matches poised, I heard a noise outside the window. Screened by long deep blue curtains and peeping through a tiny crack, I groaned as I saw the night guardian settling himself comfortably on the grass just outside. He was bound to hear the roar from the cooker. We had another look at the menu. If we all had soup and rolls in the dining room, we could top up with fruit and cheese in the bedroom later. I pushed the cooker and tell-tale tins of food into the wardrobe and we strolled off through the grounds, like any normal guests. Before leaving the dining room after our meagre supper, we ordered a 6 a.m. breakfast—the waiter winced visibly but we meant to make up for our lost day. We devastated the breakfast table once more popping all the left over rolls into my handbag before we left. David wanted to do another all night run into Tanzania.

Susan and I felt we must keep our leader fresh for the later hours of the next leg of the journey. We took the driving in turns during the morning, through the rest of Rwanda to the border, leaving David to lounge in the reclining seat and amuse the children—often much more wearing than coping with difficult roads.

The tar seal inevitably soon gave way to tough dirt roads which became more and more difficult to navigate because of numerous diversions and road works. The whole section seemed to be under repair and rebuild with lines of ugly boulders across the track—and conflicting road signs. Rain added to our difficulties and the red roads became treacherous. More than once the whole vehicle drifted sideways as we slowed to walking pace on sharp bends. Very few of the villages were tarred and the roads criss-crossed in all directions. We stopped and retraced our steps on half a dozen occasions, ignoring David's caustic comments about leaving women at the helm. Most of the workers driving their bulldozers and huge earth-moving equipment were Chinese. They smiled inscrutiably but we were unable to communicate with them and so just incredulously grinned and waved. The scale on our Michelin map was too small to be of much help and of course there was no record of all the new and half-built roads. Long stretches were almost ready for tarmac and we lumbered off the old track on to them only to be chased off a few miles further on by groups of enraged workers.

The frontier post of Kusano was closed for lunch when we finally arrived so we got out our bête noir the petrol cooker and brewed up and made pilchard sandwiches—as usual gathering a curious crowd of chatty spectators. An hour later the efficient rather serious young official stamped and cleared all our paperwork and we drove slowly across the bridge and waterfalls into Tanzania. Within five minutes we had to stop again for one of our strangest police checks so far. Susan and I donned midi-skirts having read many reports of harassment and problems due to improper dress. Frankly, we felt rather foolish after so many weeks in practical jeans—and looked slightly ridiculous as we only had boots to wear with them. Tucked away among the trees was a tiny mud hut and close by a tent. We were unsure which to approach and I stood hesitantly between the two. The young policeman on duty straightened himself and smiled broadly as he emerged through the tiny door of the hut and held out his hand. I followed him into his cramped office and crouched on the stool he offered. A transistor radio perched on the upturned box played loudly and the officer's friend beat a steady rhythm on the side of his stool. David joined us but had to crouch in the doorway, there just was not room for anyone else. We spread out all our documents and shouted above the tuneless pop music but the policeman was totally disinterested in our papers. He handed me a card recommending a curry restaurant in Mwanza, shook hands all round and told us to report at the customs post two miles down the road. "What do you think all that was about?" I asked David as we climbed aboard once more. He laughed, "You'll probably find that young man's dad owns the curry house."

A large notice at the side of the road as we approached customs explained about East African Insurance for vehicles, and all the penalties for not complying, but as Mwanza was a day and a half's drive away, there was no way we could obey the instructions for the time being. Police and customs were again housed together. We had obviously disturbed their siesta as they tumbled out of their rooms, buttoning shirts and smoothing ruffled hair, but they did not seem to mind and talked to us at length in very good English.

Crossing borders and filling in forms always absorbed a great deal of time. We drove a few miles rolling down from the hills onto the undulating plain, still very green and lush with a lot of azalea bushes but very few trees. In no time we felt we must stop and make an evening meal before our all-night drive. The road was narrow with lots of bends but eventually we found a relatively safe spot and pulled off before the quickly descending night caught up with us. Two cars and a lorry drove past, each kindly stopping to see if we were in trouble and spend a few minutes chatting and patting Sarah's blond head.

Perched on the grassy bank we drank our soup and chattered incessantly, oblivious of the formidable conditions ahead of us that night. It seemed as if someone had put together all the most dreadful patches of track as a final test for vehicle and driver. For the first few hours we crashed over bumps and corrugations and into deep fissures, gasping as the jolts threw us backwards and forwards and our seat belts threatened to cut through our bruised flesh. Each driver in turn spun the wheel this way and that in a desperate effort to avoid the worst holes and climb up over the chassis-breaking ridges. The children followed their worn pattern and curled up happily on their foam and slept, not even stirring when we stopped about 2 a.m. to make some coffee and sandwiches. Susan seemed particularly tired, she wasn't avoiding the holes, she was driving straight for them, David told me quietly—he was always her co-driver. David and I decided to share the driving and let her sleep.

The conditions deteriorated, after a long section of corrugation, reminding us once more of the desert, the track changing abruptly. The Land Rover slewed round through 90^0 and wallowed. We were in soft sand! Fortunately David was driving and quickly worked through the gears and kept us moving. We pitched and rolled and the engine screamed. I hung on to the dashboard and peered ahead into the darkness. Every one else slept soundly. Susan snorted and sought a more comfortable position as we ran back onto the bumpy corrugations once more with a sigh of relief. I grinned at David and peered ahead once more. "Oh no, look out, straight ahead" I shouted. The wavering headlights reflected in water at the bottom of the huge mud holes. We were driving into a huge mud bath, thick tenacious, reddy-brown slime just waiting to suck at our wheels and drag us into a cheerless pit. David swung the wheel wildly to the right and we drove along at a sickening angle along the side of the bank. The children slid over into a heap on the left side in the back. I looked through the window of my door and saw the dark wet earth only arm's length away. We were on a hill. We simply dare not stop. In the dark distance a faint light glimmered and a large black shape came into view on the left side of the track. Two figures approached waving their arms and beseeching us to stop but we dare not. As we drew abreast still pursuing our crazy list, I saw an enormous lorry well and truly stuck with mud half way up its side. We would never be able to pull it out—our only hope was to keep going. It was just like sailing, fighting a storm, trying to keep everything under some sort of control and keep pointing in the right direction.

I did not need to do the co-driver's job of chatting and keeping the driver awake and on the ball. David was tuned up to a very fine degree, determined to get through. I was glad everyone else was asleep, there was no back seat driving or distractions. When our tension had almost reached breaking point and the muscles in our necks and jaws threatened to remain permanently set in their grim line, it was suddenly over and we trundled back onto firm ground and assumed an upright position once more—only then did we utter a long sigh and stretch our aching arms and shoulders. I leant across and gave David a quick kiss. We both knew that if I had been at the wheel we would never have made it.

The going seemed reasonable again—well, better than it had been so I insisted on doing my stint, silently praying that there would be no more mud holes waiting round the corner. I was tired and twitchy but did my best to weave in and out of the potholes. I thought I was going very well but David suddenly told me to stop. Susan stirred and woke up, she had slept for three hours. We made more coffee and snacks. "You climb into the sleeping seat" David told me. He looked grey and exhausted. "No, you sleep and I will co-drive" I suggested. "Susan feels like driving now." "Get in and sleep" he ordered abruptly "you could hardly see to drive half an hour ago." "I know I'm too tired to drive", I shouted "but I can still co-drive", you sleep and then you will be fit to drive us onto the ferry in the morning at Mwansa. "Get in, Susan; she's going to be quite unreasonable." "Get in and sleep" I implored. "Mummy, do as Daddy tells you" said a sleepy voice from the back of the Land Rover. I peered in and saw Peter leaning on one elbow, obviously awakened by the raised voices.

I was furious, exhausted and unreasonable. I felt my logic was quite obvious. Why couldn't he understand? He was immovable. I climbed into the reclining seat, supposedly to sleep, but I seethed inwardly at his pompous male attitude and puffed quickly at a cigarette unable to settle. Why, I asked myself were men so impossible.

This was a strange situation and state of mind. David and I have always been a most equable pair—even cabbagey as described by some of our close friends. We don't argue or shout, we have always been able to agree to differ without anger. Susan was greatly amused, she told me later, she has been our friend for many years and knew better than to intervene in a situation produced by extreme fatigue and a harrowing night.

Eventually my ridiculous self righteous anger seeped away and my racing heart settled down to its normal quiet rhythm. I slid down in the seat, curled up my aching limbs and slept.

CHAPTER 12

THE WONDERS OF THE SERENGETI . . .

BRIGHT SUNLIGHT FILTERED through my puffy eyelids. I stirred and dozed for ten minutes before blinking at the new day. I wiped the dried rough saliva off my chin. "You were dribbling" laughed Susan. I tried to focus. "Where are we?" My tongue was dry, thick and foul. "At the ferry at Mwanza, you went out like a light." "How's David?" I asked anxiously. "He's fine, just negotiating our crossing." All around us was a busy bustling crowd, sleepy babies slung on their mothers' backs and wide eyed children staring in through the windows. I wiped my face with a cologne tissue and moved into the front to listen to Susan's description of the beautiful sunrise over the glassy calm Lake Victoria. I was sorry I had missed it.

The ferry was highly efficient and well organised. We were in the wide modern streets of Mwanza by 9.30 a.m. "First stop at the bank" said David "then we must arrange our insurance." We found a parking slot in the main street and Susan and David crossed the busy road, passports and travellers cheques at the ready. Half an hour later there was no sign of them. "I have to go to the loo Mummy" said Sean. I scanned both sides of the street but could not see a likely spot. "You'll have to nip up that little side road and see what you can find." Sean climbed out followed by Peter and Sarah, now they all wanted to go.

Meanwhile in the bank, David and Susan jostled for a place at the counter but could not defeat the African system of no queue. The one desk clerk merely selected a customer from the crowd in front of him but it was never them. In the end they gave up and walked across to a pretty girl working quietly at her desk and begged her to help them. Pens poised ready to complete the forms they both paused with embarrassed smiles.

"Can you tell us what day it is and the date?" David asked apologetically. We had been living in our happy world of limbo for so long that these little details had lost all importance. Our everyday problems had become very basic—feeding hungry children, finding a place to sleep and seeking new places and people to broaden our vision of the world.

The children seemed to have been gone for a very long time. I was just locking the last door when they arrived back breathless and laughing. "We had to walk miles, simply miles, and then we think it was a man's garden" they spluttered giggling and nudging each other. "Get in quickly" I said, "here's Daddy coming. Let's go before someone tries to prosecute us." Now we had money we could buy our insurance and petrol—and perhaps an early lunch. I pulled out the card advertising the curry house and told everyone to look out for Station Road. We found the road, but not the restaurant and had to make do with a sleazy coffee bar before tumbling out onto the open road again. It was very hot. We were unwashed, sticky and very tired.

Stopping to pick up bread and bananas on the outskirts of the town we measured the distance to the border camp of the Serengeti game park and decided we could make it by mid-afternoon. The road was fairly smooth. It was obviously a fairly major highway passing through many collections of houses each with their central compound of washing facilities and running taps. The soft whispering whistle of the wheels on the tarmac settled us like a lullaby. One after another our heads sank lower and lower and heavy eyes fought to stay open. We suddenly jerked awake as David pulled up onto the rough verge and stopped in a hurry.

"I can't stay awake. I have to rest for an hour" he said and we all climbed out into the sparse shade of an old tree. The sun twinkled through the brown shrivelled leaves overhead as we stretched out on dusty short grass. Sweat trickled down inside our shirts but sleep was the stronger master. Dreamless oblivion crashed in like a blow on the head. "Get up, get up quickly" the children shook us roughly by the shoulders. Light-headed and slightly disoriented we scrambled to our feet and stumbled onto the road as a local herdsman drove his oxen across our humble bed. We had slept for half an hour. That was that, we might as well move on.

We arrived at the gate of the Serengeti Game Park about 4 in the afternoon. David seemed to take an age paying the camping fees. He finally walked out of the little office scowling. The charges were absolutely ridiculous—$1.40 per head to camp—every 24 hours! We drove through the barrier into the so-called campsite which really did not exist. It was left to us to select a spot, totally unprotected from the animals. There was no water, merely one tiny shack which was a combined rubbish tip and dry loo. We had only half a container of water left and viewed the prospect with some misgivings.

Having selected a site, we unhitched the trailer, turned the children loose with lots of warnings about straying too far and David decided to head back to a village nearby to get more water. The official refused to let him through the gate. If he went out it would be closing time when he got back and they would not let him in again. He explained about our water and he very reluctantly gave him another half full container. Our beer supply had long since been exhausted—two crates to help us out of many a difficult situation and the rest shared and drunk with the many fascinating people we had met along the way. We had tried to buy some more but as we had always discarded our empty bottles, we were completely beaten by the African system which involved the exchange of one empty bottle each time you bought a full one. Try as we did, we could not find out how you started off the chain, short of stealing a few empty bottles. In exasperation, David produced a bottle of port which he had bought somewhere along the way. It was rather early for port and we had empty stomachs. Supper was still sizzling or bubbling in the saucepans, but we were past caring. We each sank a large glass of the sweet sickly liquid. It quickly caught up with our fatigue and made us light headed and slightly silly.

In the far distance we could see gazelles and a small herd of zebra and then a movement in the bushes much nearer to us caught my eye and I called urgently to the children to come back to the vehicle. A large baboon lolloped into view and made straight for us. We backed away from the table as he ignored my shooing noises and Susan started climbing up the ladder onto the roof rack. "I wouldn't go up there if I were you" I laughed "It will be up there in one spring and then you are stuck. I can tell by the gleam in his eye he especially likes the look of you." She giggled nervously and backed down the ladder staying close to the Land Rover for a quick escape. I tried waving my arms and shouting but the animal was undeterred, only pausing for a moment to bare its teeth, sniff with disdain and then with one leap reached the table grabbed the bananas and bounded back a few feet. With a big toothy coarse laugh it tossed its head, expertly peeled the bananas and gobbled them up before we had time to comment. As the children squeaked and hopped about, the baboon slowly approached us again looking for more supper. A small group of its friends collected a short way off and watched nervously. David grabbed the fire extinguisher and fired two short burst at the precocious uninvited guest. It backed away, made a very rude noise and watched from a safe distance. "My word, look at his knockers!" exclaimed Sarah. "Darling!" I cried in a shocked voice "where did you learn that expression?" "Oh, the boys and I use it all the time" she replied nonchalantly. "So much for all those school fees I've been paying to a school for *young ladies*." I winked at David and let it pass.

I quickly served supper, anxious to get everyone into an early bed. We decided to sleep out again but with the children safely inside the Land Rover, of course. As usual Susan took a sleeping tablet and tucked in her mosquito net. "Don't wake me" she instructed "except in case of dire emergency, like breakfast is getting cold or something equally important." I was always very privileged and had the middle spot, sleeping between Susan and David and protected on either side. I always teased them that they didn't want to lose their cook and bottle washer!

Susan slept soundly throughout the night oblivious of the wandering night life. A huge hippopotamus snorted and grazed around us and many unidentified pairs of eyes inspected us and strolled by. David and I did our hourly vigil throughout the hours of darkness, wary but unafraid. We believed that healthy wild animals do not seek out people as long as both treat each other with respect and care, but we did not feel that the same rule applied to children, and later had this confirmed by a very highly qualified vet. Wild animals instinctively recognize the vulnerability of a child and will continue to approach and probably attack. I was worried about Sean and his typical small male capacity bladder and slept with one ear and one eye open so that I could supervise his nocturnal journeys.

We woke up slowly to a lovely red mackerel sky, everyone feeling greatly rested and content. A brief breakfast, quick pack-up and we started to drive through the game reserve well after first light and fearing that we might be too late to see many animals. We were confounded and utterly delighted, first speechless and then more than a little loquacious, with the beautiful and breath-taking selection of animals and creatures we saw along the 80 mile stretch from the Western Gate to the Central Seronera camping area. Pretty Thompson and Grants gazelles with their flicking tails leapt gracefully and provocatively across the track as we approached. Huge herds of wildebeest thundered across the plain, trailing behind them a thick dust cloud whilst heavy broad shouldered buffaloes raised their heads momentarily and then continued to graze. "There's a giraffe" shouted Sarah pointing at a group of trees. It stretched its long neck and nibbled leaves. Tiny birds perched precariously on its willowy neck, pecking busily at the flies and small insects which lived in its short hairy coat.

The children were excited; they had waited so long to see the animals. Every few minutes someone would shout "Look! Look!". We all scanned the bushes and grassland eagerly, each hoping to outdo the rest with a new exciting find. Mean, mangy looking hyenas slunk out of the large drainage pipes along the side of the track and pretty bat-eared foxes popped up startled heads and inquisitive eyes. We all laughed loudly at the families of warthogs—mum, dad and babies—as they ran off into the distance with their flagpole tails, stiff and erect. We ooh'd and aah'd at the distinguished, gorgeous marabou storks standing like old men, stooped with imaginary hands clasped behind their backs. It was a wonderful, wonderful morning, we revelled and marvelled and gasped at the beauty of nature and felt our journey had been well worthwhile.

In the Seronera, the buildings were very scattered. Up one winding track was the campsite but with no facilities at all, not even water. Along another, lay a luxurious hotel frequented by wealthy overseas visitors who flew in to the small airstrip. Driving around and following the rather confusing road signs, we eventually found the hotel which we were really looking for and which cost very little more per head than the camp site and was excellent. Financed many years ago by an American, it comprised a long one-storey building full of beds and across a tiny yard at the back, showers and toilets. There was even a small kitchen with a solid fuel cooker if one felt that enthusiastic. We decided to rest for a couple of days and enjoy this lovely place.

We unpacked, relaxed and wallowed for a few hours, but then the terrible anxiety of feeling that we may be missing something overcame us and David drove over to the administration office and organised a guide for a couple of hours in the afternoon. We left the trailer at the hostel and the guide drove us across open country and away from the orthodox tracks. He knew just where to go and where to look. We stopped only a few yards away from a large pride of lions, panting and resting near a water hole. Their bellies were round and bulging they had obviously fed fairly recently and regarded us with total disdain and disinterest, only stirring to find a more comfortable position or stroll over to the water hole to squat and lap noisily. Father was nowhere to be seen but we came across him later with another younger male looking magnificent and proud as he squinted in the bright sun and watched us closely. "Look, there in that tree" said our guide suddenly pointing over to the right. We all swung our heads round and looked expectantly. "I can't see anything" said Sean. "Neither can I" I admitted. "It's a leopard" said the guide. We all looked again and sure enough, stretched along the branch among the leaves quite motionless was a leopard. Without a keen-eyed guide, we would have driven straight past. All around us roamed zebra, gazelles and giraffes. It was beautiful, breath-taking and quite lovely.

As we turned to make our way back to the offices, the guide suddenly slammed on the brakes and reversed quickly pointing to another tree very close to the edge of the track. There was another leopard with a freshly killed Thompson gazelle sprawled over the fork of the trunk. A casual observer would have missed it as it blended perfectly with the colouring of the bark and leaves only the twitch and curl of its tail as it tore huge hunks of meat off the hind quarters gave away its presence. We watched fascinated, staring into its indifferent, expressionless, eyes. What a wonderful day we had all had.

Two more groups of people had arrived at the hostel when we returned and they all inspected our Land Rover and gear with interest and chatted to the children. As always they were soon consulting David about their own truck problems. They rightly assumed he must be quite an expert to bring this happy band of women and children so far and still have a vehicle in first class running order.

Before beginning the big supper cook-up we showered, changed, and drove across to the hotel for cold beers. It was built into the side of a huge unevenly shaped rock, large hunks still protruding into the elegant dining room which led down into a large cocktail lounge with long windows looking out over the rolling plain. Gripping our cold glasses, we watched the reddening glow of the sky with it's sinking fiery sun. The hazy skyline sharpened and cleared, only broken by the charcoal etchings of passing giraffes along with the curved horns of the buffalo.

It was rather a noisy night in the communal dormitory, with an Indian family, hawking, spitting, and chattering in the background and everyone having to walk through our screened section to get to the loo. We made up for it by lounging and lazing late in the morning.

True to pattern we embarked on a workday. David and the boys changed the Land Rover tyres and gave it a thorough service and clean while Susan and I compulsively washed and repacked everything in the trailer. By this stage of the journey we had both developed a deep unreasonable hatred for the trailer. Everything in it was filthy, disgusting and depressing. We would quite cheerfully have put a match to the lot except that our good sense prevailed and we again did our best to preserve the remains of our depleted food supply. We had successfully fed six people every day and still had enough left for a few more weeks. I am quite sure however that without Susan to help me, there would have been the odd occasion when I would have resorted to a few quiet tears over the general state of things and breakages.

We all worked until the late afternoon and in the hot sun felt ready to drop. Showers washed away the grime and we stretched out on our beds to gather new energy. The children served us with coffee and biscuits—always most thoughtful when they saw we were tired, and we held a family conference about our plans for the next few days. Refreshed and relaxed we dragged out the suitcases, put on long skirts and suits and drove over to the hotel for dinner—David felt it was time we all had a treat.

A good night's sleep seemed to be something which eluded David and me throughout the entire journey. Two hours after we switched off the light and muttered our goodnights, the thunder rumbled in the distance and then broke with a resounding crash over our heads. The rain came down and close by the lions roared with disgust or delight—we didn't know which. I fought to make an exit out of my mosquito net and tiptoed across to David's bed and snuggled in. I wondered if I would ever sleep through a whole night again.

We crept quietly through the dormitory before dawn and stowed our luggage in the cool and sweet smelling first light. Susan stacked a load of rubbish and walked round the back of the hostel to the bin. She reappeared two minutes later, running and glancing over her shoulder. A large hyena slunk away into the bushes. We all peered around cautiously after that. "Children, come and look" I called, bending down to examine the wet earth. Lion paw marks were clearly imprinted everywhere, our late night noisy visitors!

Driving eastwards we left the Serengeti and headed towards the Ngorongoro crater, passing through large herds of zebra and buck. As we rolled across the plain we saw a barrier ahead and eased to a halt. The guardian told us we were now approaching the area of the Olduvai Gorge and must pay another $1.30 per head plus $1.40 per person to camp. We always seemed to be putting our hands in our pocket.

It was too good an opportunity to miss. As we trundled along the bumpy road, we tried briefly and simply to tell the children about Dr. Leakey and his discoveries, meeting a lot of opposition from Sarah Jane as we dispelled her belief in Adam and Eve. Seeing a signpost we swung off to the left and wound our way along to the little museum and excavation sites. The guided tour was way over the children's heads and we adults confessed to being a bit confused, but at least the children understood the basic idea and were awed at the sight of the deep gorge in the Rift Valley and gathered lumps of lava as mementos when we visited the excavation sites.

Off once more, the road climbed steeply to seven and a half thousand feet, winding around the hillsides like narrow strips of ribbon. A few Masai with their herds of cattle, free to graze in the conservation area around the Ngorongoro Crater and safe from the tsetse fly, paused and watched our progress.

Our first glimpse of the crater left us speechless. We stopped and gazed down through a break in the hills and were confounded. Eager to see more, we quickly drove on to find the camp and organise a tour. The road wound forever upwards with sharp bends and overhanging branches and the weather closed in. Spots of rain left dusty smears down the windscreen and light fluffy mist hovered round us like a cocoon. Eventually we found the office and presented our camping tickets bought 40 miles previously, but were met by sour faces and shaking heads. They would not allow us to camp at the site, it was too dangerous. There had been a lot of trouble with some of the Masai, the official told us, not just thieving, and women and children would be in danger. David and I went into a huddle. "We'll organise a trip down into the crater, get our camping fees back and drive on" he told me. I agreed, we could not sleep there if there was real risk to the children. David went back to the official at the desk. "We can't refund your camping fees" he said "you must go back to the gate where you bought them." "But that's 40 miles away" retorted David. The official shrugged his shoulders. "It would destroy our accounts system" he replied. We bit back the sharp reply which leapt to our lips and asked for a guide to take us into the crater in our Land Rover. There followed another head shaking session. We would have to go in an African Land Rover and it would cost $20. We turned on our heels and marched out of the office. The rain was falling steadily and visibility was poor. "Forget it" I told David "this is all getting too expensive for words." "Let's go" he said firmly, and climbed into the Land Rover. "We still have to find somewhere to sleep tonight."

We all felt very disappointed and rather disgruntled about all the red tape. As we wound our way slowly down from the dizzy heights, we caught momentary glimpses of the lake in the centre of the crater and the lush vegetation, and then paused to chat to a group of Masai and admire their beautiful beaded collars and bracelets.

The map was getting a bit tattered and grubby. We smoothed it gently lest it fell into pieces where the many folds had started to separate and the edges curled over. However we had only one more stop before reaching Kenya, so it was all over bar the shouting.

Arusha in Tanzania had wide streets and lots of modern shops. We half looked for a hotel, but mostly for a coffee bar. A little place next to the garage served us delicious toasted cheese and tomato sandwiches and large cups of steaming coffee. The melting butter ran down our fingers and we licked and sucked, seemingly having forgotten all our table manners, but in fact relishing the treat and reluctant to waste one mouthful. We wiped our greasy fingers, downed another cup of coffee and decided to drive on to Moshi and find a hotel—that would leave a fairly short run next day.

As the miles slowly clicked by on our last lap of the day, we saw towering in the distance the much talked about and ever beautiful snow-capped peak of Kilimanjaro. I felt a very personal sense of triumph and deep pleasure having secretly set the first sight of the mountain as my private goal when we had begun our rugged journey. I was more than rewarded for my sleepless nights and moments of nerve-stretching anxiety.

We easily found a little hotel, and for the first time since leaving home, slept right through the night. In the early morning I drew back the curtains, looked up at the majestic mountain and the sun peeped around the craggy slopes and winked.

Only a few miles out of Moshi the Land Rover shook and resounded with our cheers and noisy laughter. The stained truck whistled over the smooth surface and we all looked at David apprehensively as we gathered speed—but we were only doing 50 mph. It felt very fast after our weeks of slow bumpy progress. "Welcome to Kenya" read Peter as we approached the border. "Welcome to Kenya" we murmured, all hugging and kissing each other.

CHAPTER 13

A BIRTHDAY IN AFRICA, THEN TIME TO HEAD HOME . . .

"LEFT IS TO the hills, right to the seaside, which is it going to be, children?" "Seaside! Seaside!" they shouted with one voice. We were at a major T-Junction, turning onto the Nairobi-Mombasa highway. We turned right, following the arrow to Mombasa. It was February 3rd, just two months since we had left Kent, and we had safely driven almost 9,000 miles. None of us ever religious, but I think we all said a silent prayer of thanks.

Mombasa was busy, noisy, humid and hot. David tried to remember to give traffic signals and look in his driving mirror. The cars seemed to drive very quickly and weave in and out dangerously, hooting their horns continuously while pedestrians made a mad dash for the pavements. We were hungry and thirsty but we had a problem. The banks were shut and we had no Kenyan money. David spied a shady parking spot in a line of cars along one of the main streets and we squeezed in, although the trailer stuck out at an awkward angle into the road. We all climbed out and stretched and wilted in the oppressive heat.

"Keep an eye on our gear" David told us "I'll be back in a minute." We leant against the hot doors of the truck, mopping our faces with tissues and looking longingly at the tall cool drinks on the tables of the Wimpey bar close by. I pumped some water through the filter. It was warm and flat but better than nothing. David came striding determinedly back and we moved towards him expectantly. "Have you got any money?" I asked hopefully. "Not yet" he replied "but it shouldn't take long, I met a man who knows a man . . . ." I laughed before he finished the sentence, he was never beaten for long! "We'll go and look at the menu in the Wimpey bar" I told him. "Just work up an appetite, see you there."

He disappeared through a doorway and down into a basement. When he joined us we had already ordered such was our faith in his ability to solve all our problems. He put down a large bundle of tourist brochures on the table and as we dolloped tomato ketchup on what we had chosen and sipped cold lemonade, we thumbed through them, looking for a spot by the sea.

Weeks ago in Nigeria a fellow camper had recommended a place called Twiga Lodge. We found it among the glossy pictures and decided to go and have a look. We wanted a base, for at least a week, perhaps longer, to rest and relax and think back over the previous few weeks.

Mombasa is built on an island—joined to the mainland either by causeways or ferries. We were heading south so lined up in the queue for one of the ferries back to the mainland, leaning out of the windows to buy ice creams from a strategically placed van as we sat in the simmering heat.

Only a few hundred yards after driving off the ferry at the other side we saw a camping sign. We might as well look, we had plenty of time. Turning down the narrow, sandy bumpy road we passed a few private houses here and there, and a couple of hotels but Susan and I shook our heads firmly when David lifted an enquiring eyebrow, it was too expensive for six people to stay in a hotel. Ideally, we had decided, we wanted a beach hut or small house, a happy compromise between tent and hotel. Winding around numerous bends we finally arrived at a bare square patch of sand enclosed by a high wire fence with a broken faded camping sign. There was a tiny 6' x 6' hut at the gateway selling bits of this and that, otherwise it was empty. The children leapt out all ready to pitch tent there and then but Susan, David and I wrinkled our noses and called them back. There was still a few hours of daylight left and we decided to look further. On our way back to the main road we pulled in at a children's' holiday hotel with houses built round a central playground complete with swings and seesaws. I peeped in through the office window when no-one answered my knock, but it was empty. Suddenly a chord rang out from an electric organ and deft fingers ran up and down the keys. I followed the sound of the music and found the proprietor in his lounge, deaf to my knocks until he came to the end of his piece. He showed us a small house for hire and teased and congratulated the children on their journey. It seemed ideal, the cool wind from the Indian Ocean dried our sweating bodies and blew through our hair. The palms bowed and rustled and the white waves broke gently on the shore. The three children looked at us with happy shining eyes. Susan's mouth was set firmly, drooping slightly at the corners, saying nothing. Although adoring and marvellous with my three children, she heartily disliked large groups of children and each house was occupied by a family with at least two or more little ones. This was not her idea of heaven.

I nudged David, told my three now slightly disgruntled offspring to get back into the Land Rover and promised the proprietor we would return if we did not like Twiga—only half an hour down the road. "Why couldn't we stay Mummy?" complained Sean and Sarah as we bowled down the tarmac road once more. I made soothing noises and winked at Susan. She had worked jolly hard throughout the trip and put up with all my family's funny ways. She deserved a good rest and opportunity to escape if she wanted to. "There's a sign post" shouted Sarah, face flushed and hair plastered to her small head. We all sat quite still for a few moments after we had drawn to a halt at Twiga Lodge. This had to be it. The children moved first, flinging open the doors and leaving them swinging wide as they rushed down the steps onto the white sand. A trail of hard smelly socks and discarded boots pointed the way to the blue sea and soft rippling foam. We knew we could not ask them to go one step further.

There was a beach hut for hire with three bedrooms, kitchen, bathroom and large veranda. At the bottom of the slope only a few yards from the beach was a small shop, restaurant, bar and library—absolutely ideal for everyone's requirements. We booked the house, parked the Land Rover and flipped the tops of three bottles of iced beer. We had arrived! It seemed impossible, quite incredible, already like a dream, but there we were, feet up sipping cold beer, weathered faces creased with triumphant smiles, listening to the delighted shrieks from the children as they splashed into the Indian Ocean.

Supper was a little late. We moved down to the bar and sank a few more beers before I could muster the energy to dig into the trailer and put a match to the cooker, which lit instantly instead of spluttering and making vulgar noises like our camping stove. No one seemed to mind the late hour. Eventually we stacked the dishes and fell into bed. As darkness fell, the chattering of the monkeys in the overhanging trees stopped abruptly, only the crickets and the whispering palms played a soothing melody to the accompanying swoosh of the waves up the beach.

We slept soundly and deeply between the white sheets and were woken by gentle kisses from Peter, Sean and Sarah. They had made us coffee and toast and cuddled into our beds with "thank you's" for a wonderful journey. We returned their kisses and thanked them. They had really been fantastic, working hard and accepting all the responsibilities we had heaped on their young shoulders. They had adapted readily to hard and sometimes hazardous conditions with a frightening faith in our ability to overcome and solve any problems. We felt they had noticeably matured and expanded their already easy manner and respect when dealing with people and learnt a great deal that the books at school would never have taught them. "Now we are going to have a holiday" I grinned, leaping out of bed, forgetting that I had resorted to my home habit of sleeping 'starkers' instead of in long john pyjamas and socks. "Mummy, think of the monkeys!" laughed Peter, grabbing a sheet and winding it round me. I did a sexy dance through the large airy bedroom and the children joined in, wobbling their bottoms and giggling. "Let's swim" shrieked Sean, suddenly dashing off, followed hot foot by the other two. They rummaged through their grimy dusty sail bags, flinging clothes in all directions as they searched for their trunks. Grabbing towels they ran down the steps, yelping as the sharp stones stuck into their feet, and down onto the beach. David followed while I searched for something more suitable to wear than a sheet and thought about breakfast.

It felt wrong not hastily packing up, searching around for forgotten articles and setting off for another long day's drive. Susan and I wandered aimlessly through the kitchen, stamping on the unwelcome ants and generally surveying the scene. I turned on the tap, but it did not flow, just trickled. So I rushed through the rather basic bathroom, put the plug in the bath and turned on the tap. I had learnt a lot during our travels, get as much water as you can when you can!

We settled into a happy relaxed life of sea, sun and sleep. There was still enough food in the trailer to feed us for a couple of weeks and despite everyone's groans and moans I insisted that we ate it. The whole journey has cost us quite a lot more than we had expected. Petrol had been £1 a gallon most of the way instead of the 50p on which we had based our original calculations. We were already dipping into the money we had estimated would pay for our air tickets home and would have to send a telegram for more.

After 24 hours, David in his usual restless fashion went off to explore more of the coast. He returned some three hours later—and I hardly need say it. He had met a man—an Englishman by the name of Elkan, a writer for the Sunday Times—who knew a man who might want to buy our Land Rover. If you are not married to a person like David, you may not appreciate that unless you wear a pair of roller skates—physically and mentally, it is almost impossible to keep up with the changing scene of life as he likes it. I am sure it was this spark, a magic untouchable quality and determination to conquer the world that captured me at the tender age of 20. I vainly perhaps like to think that just a little of it has rubbed off and rounded some of the corners of my North Country common sense. Ours is a love story, this journey merely an exciting fleeting moment in the racing years. "Now this man who knows a man", I winked at Susan who spread her hands in disbelief. "Are we going to meet him?" "Oh yes" said David, throwing himself into a chair, "he should be here in a few minutes with his wife and toddler." I leapt to my feet, gathering up a stack of dirty cups and plates and brushing the dust off the table with my forearm.

Jeffrey, David's partner, had already sent out advertisements from England to the newspapers in Nairobi in the hopes of finding a customer for the Land Rover but there was nothing like personal contact. Elkan gave us the telephone number of his friend and we promised to look him up. We were anxious to sell, as the market at home sounded flat and shipping costs were very expensive.

Susan and David left very early next morning to go into Mombasa and find a bank. We needed to change money and arrange about the import duty for the vehicle. The rest of us swam and lounged and tried to settle to some school work but the heat was unbelievable and the humidity quite exhausting. By 10 a.m. we were reduced to wet, wilting, bedraggled figures. Any work or travelling had to be confined to the early morning or late evenings. It was as much as we could do to stagger down to the beach and flop into the shallow water.

The bang of the Land Rover door woke me from uneasy siesta stretched out on crumpled sheets, with pools of perspiration collecting in the creases round my middle. There seemed to be a lot of voices. Susan led three young men up the steps onto the veranda and introduced them. They were pilots from the U.S.S. Enterprise which together with the Q.E. II had docked in Mombasa the previous day. The town apparently was heaving with people from the two ships and all prices had doubled and trebled overnight. These young men wanted nothing more than to stretch out on the beach and swim so David had brought them back to spend the day with us. They more than repaid our hospitality by telling the boys long exciting tales of their activities and adventures aboard ship. We all sat in a huddle on the beach and the children listened wide-eyed and open mouthed all afternoon.

Two days later, after a similar trip into Mombasa, David brought us back another guest—John, an American school teacher. John had just completed the same journey as ourselves across Africa with one of the big overland groups and had hated every minute of it. Their truck had broken down time after time, their food had been dreadful and inadequate, but most of all he told us how the clash of personalities in such a big group had made it thoroughly unpleasant. We could well imagine the situation. We had observed a number of these large groups of young people and felt it must be more than a little difficult to blend together so many different people from such varying backgrounds. Some of John's tales made our toes curl; we felt lucky to have been totally independent and a well mixed team.

John stayed with us for a few days and was joined by his friend Phil. They planned to sail across to India and hitch hike, but first hoped to climb Kilimanjaro. I desperately wanted to go up the mountain with them, but felt we were running out of time and must soon be thinking about moving back to Nairobi.

Strung down the coast from Twiga was a collection of luxurious hotels, with swimming pools and excellent food. It was Sarah's birthday, she was nine. So we gathered up all our swimming gear and drove along to Trade Winds to spend the day there as her treat. I had a quick word in the Manager's ear as soon as we arrived. "Happy birthday to you" sang the chef and waiters as they proudly carried out a delicious looking gateau with nine twinkling, pink candles. Sarah flushed with excitement and pleasure as she blew out the candles and made her wish—something to do with Africa she confided. In the evening there was a display of dancing. The steady throbbing rhythm of the drums and stamping feet of the dancers in the dust seemed to rock the very ground on which we stood. Sarah will never forget her African birthday!

Susan and I wanted to do an ostrich act, pretending that the nasty, disgusting trailer was not sitting outside the kitchen, but there was no escaping the last major unpack and scraping out of the brown solidified mess and then sorting through the few remaining tins. No one dare mention the word evaporated milk, we never, ever wanted to see another tin. After long chats about the pro's and con's, we had decided not to sell the trailer, but to pack it with our beds, sleeping bags, tent and all our luggage not immediately needed then ship it back to England. We estimated that the cost of replacing all our equipment would be much greater than the shipping cost. We hired a couple of local lads to help us with the scrubbing and washing but even so it was a slow process. The temperature and humidity increased daily and for the first time we had to admit to being almost beaten by the climate. The climax came one afternoon when David returned rather promptly from the beach. The sea water was too hot for swimming! He took a thermometer down to the shore and the sea water registered 100^0 F. We would have to head back north. Nairobi by all accounts enjoyed a delightful climate, being on much higher ground.

Susan decided to go by train and spend a week with some friends. David and I planned to drive and perhaps stop off along the way. We had met a lot of young people at Twiga who spoke enthusiastically about Lamu, an island off the coast just north of Malindi. Two American boys who had entertained us with their guitar playing hitched a lift with us and we regretfully waved goodbye to Twiga, left the trailer with the shipping agents in Mombasa and started northwards.

On the way to Malindi we sorted out our plans. I suddenly longed to have two or three days complete rest from cooking and washing dirty jeans. We decided to split, with David taking the boys to Lamu for snorkelling and fishing, while Sarah and I would stay on the mainland in a hotel. Sarah preened herself, she seemed to be developing a few delusions of grandeur and the thought of staying in a hotel at the seaside appealed to her very much.

Malindi was a nice little spot, with a row of luxurious hotels, mainly full of Germans, straggled along a rather wild stretch of beach. The sand was coarser, not the fine white face powder variety we had found further south, and a strong cool breeze swept in from the pounding breakers. I was quite relieved when the first three hotels could not give us a room. They looked much too exotic and expensive. Even the Sinbad which offered us a delightful twin bedroom was too pretentious for our needs, but David insisted. "You've earned it" he said. "Put your feet up and make the most of it."

In reply to his enquiries, the desk clerk told David that it was relatively cheap to fly over to Lamu and much less wearing than driving on up the coast and crossing by ferry. So off he went with the boys to find out more about the planes and find a little boarding house for the night. Sarah and I strolled off to our room and unpacked our meagre collection of clothes, hardly suitable for a top notch hotel but we would have to make do. David had promised to return and have dinner with us. As I lowered one foot into the deep, hot bath water the telephone rang at the side of my bed. "Your husband asked me to 'phone you" said the voice at the other end. "He left ten minutes ago with your two sons on an aeroplane to Lamu." "Thank you" I replied, there did not seem anything else to say. I looked at my watch; it was only forty minutes since he had left us! The speed at which David moved still left me breathless on occasions.

Sarah and I smoothed the creases in our long skirts, flicked our newly washed hair into provocative curls and went down to the moon gardens to watch another display of dancing—much better than the one we had seen a few days earlier. We smiled at each other as our feet tapped to the rhythm of the drums, keeping one eye on the dining room and wishing it would open as our tummies rumbled and complained.

Dinner was a long enjoyable affair. We worked our way through the seven courses relaxing and chattering like two old friends meeting after a long time. Sarah at only nine was a delightful companion and one of my very best friends.

Whilst the two of us whiled away the hours strolling along the beach and toasting ourselves by the pool, our menfolk explored Lamu. "Why don't you two boys be quiet for half an hour?" complained an English voice from the room next door "I'm trying to sleep." Peter and Sean paused and looked at each other and giggled. They tiptoed out of their room and down to the water's edge. "I think we owe you an apology for disturbing you" said David as he bumped into the man emerging from the door next to his that evening. They sauntered down to the bar in the Peponie hotel and sat chatting over a few drinks. A tall, well-built man in his fifties, Bill turned out to be a director of British Leyland, East Africa. "You're not by any chance the family who drove overland and now have a Land Rover for sale?" he asked. David nodded. "Well I'll be damned!" exploded Bill. "My close friend Bob Campbell in Nairobi is the chap who is interested in buying it! He told me to keep an eye open in case we came across you." At about the same moment in time, I was standing in the foyer of the Sinbad hotel, waiting patiently for my call to Nairobi. David had left me the telephone number of our prospective buyer and told me to have a preliminary talk with him and arrange to meet.

David and I compared notes two days later when he and the boys returned from Lamu to spend the night at our hotel. We all had a lot of news to catch up with and chattered incessantly throughout dinner. The boys were stimulated and excited by their flight in a small aircraft. "The pilot actually let Daddy fly us across there" they told me proudly. "But you can't fly a 'plane' I exclaimed, looking at him aghast." "I can now" he laughed.

They had all loved Lamu with its narrow streets and beautifully carved doors. There was only one motor vehicle on the island and even at that, a fairly new introduction for their medical officer. Each morning it was washed and polished and put on display. David described the feeling of stepping off the plane, and finding the clock turned back a hundred years. Telling of their fascinating sail in an original Indian Ocean dhow, he had been mystified by the fact that they could sail in so close to the island in such shallow water and wondered what they used for a keel. The mystery was soon solved when they all climbed aboard and the sails flapped in the strong breeze. There was no keel. Instead there were a number of sacks of sand used as ballast, which the crew moved around the boat to counterbalance the wind pressure on the tall lateen sails. I listened with envy, as sailing is one of our family hobbies and very sadly, I had missed out.

Our holiday by the sea was over, we had just ten days left before our flight back to England and needed to put our minds to selling the vehicle and putting our affairs in order. We sadly waved goodbye to the Indian ocean and drove first south towards Mombasa, before swinging across to join the main highway north to Nairobi. There was no point in doing a marathon drive, so we took it gently through the beautiful country. As the road wound through the game reserve, "Elephants" I shouted, pointing towards a group of trees. We had not seen any in the Serengeti and the children had almost given up hope. Many of them were reddish brown instead of the expected grey, presumably because of the brick red earth. We watched hopefully for more animals, but only saw giraffe and the bleached powdery looking trunks of the dead trees which the elephants had devastated.

We spent the night at Hunters Lodge, leaving us with a morning's run into Nairobi. The difference in the climate was very noticeable. The humidity level had dropped remarkably and although very warm in the middle of the day, we no longer felt exhausted and limp. Cars seemed to drive at us from every direction and with such speed and reckless abandon that we cringed and hugged the pavement, trying to adjust. Afterwards we tried to analyse this feeling and decided that after driving on empty tracks for so many weeks we had lost our aggression. If a car tried to edge alongside us, we invariably gave way, often finding ourselves in the wrong lane and being edged out even further. It was a little bit like going out on the road for the first time after passing your driving test.

We had booked in at a hotel by telephone, but re-negotiated the rooms when we arrived. We were scraping the bottom of the barrel and a whole week in a hotel might prove the last straw. For less than half the price in the main hotel, they offered us accommodation in the annex. We accepted it without even taking a look, we knew we would be able to manage. It was perfect. Actually built around a tiny square, the annex looked like a collection of old English cottages with bougainvillea straggling up the white walls. Behind the tiny wooden doors, the rooms with their bare planked floors and simple furniture were all that we required. Attached to the hotel was a club with swimming pool and gardens. The children quickly made friends with others in the hotel and we barely saw them as they swam and played for hours on end.

Within minutes of arriving a man approached David. He had seen our advertisement in the newspaper for the Land Rover and wanted to buy it. After a quick inspection he was ready to pay the money there and then. He was an American working with a local mission and desperately wanted the vehicle because of the aluminium body—as opposed to the steel body of his present Japanese Land Cruiser which tended to rust in the East African climate.

The other important features he admired were the four doors and 6 cylinder capacity. The only approaching equivalent buy on the East African market was a two door, 4 cylinder model. It was very tempting, to part with it, remembering the old 'bird in the hand' philosophy, but we had promised to contact Bob Campbell as soon as we arrived and give him first refusal. We felt morally obliged to keep our promise.

Throughout our entire trip we had only seen two snakes, and those very briefly as they slithered across the road. I tramped off to the snake park with the three children to spend a couple of hours cringing and uttering exclamations of horror and physical disgust as I watched them feed on whole, live chickens and frogs. David meanwhile met up with Bob, a charming, quietly spoken man. The kind of person one grossly underestimates on first meeting. He was a photographer, and had taken many films for the Geographical Society and for some of the wild life series that we had watched on the television at home.

When we subsequently drove out to his home and met Heather his wife, who was a vet, she had fascinating tales to tell us of how she had been responsible for caring for the animals in the making of films like Born Free, we knew we had met a rare couple. Quiet and unassuming they were a fund of knowledge on the animal and plant life of Africa. Heather had exotic flowers and plants growing everywhere in and around their ideally placed bungalow, looking out over the hills and large greenhouses filled with beautiful, delicately poised orchids, but what gripped us most of all were their pet hyrax—hamster-like creatures with miniature elephant-styled feet, and highly intelligent to boot. At first I was slightly taken aback when I heard they lived freely in Heather's bedroom and then astounded when I learnt that these small creatures opened the door themselves and trotted through to the bathroom when they wanted to spend a penny—perching on the toilet seat in a very human fashion.

Bob showed us superb pictures of gorillas and told us about a three year study he had recently completed in the mountains of Rwanda. He had lived with the gorillas continuously and after eighteen months, having mimicked their behaviour and walked on all fours, they accepted him and allowed him to move freely amongst them. Some of his photographs were fantastic. We longed to see his films, but they were the property of the Geographical Society and not his to show to the public.

We enjoyed our peaceful hours with Bob and Heather, but most of our days were spent in clearing and sorting out the Land Rover. David dashed about trying to buy a new speedometer cable and replace odd bits and pieces which had worn out on the journey. Bill from Leyland joined us one morning to take David to see an interesting car. He related how on his flight back from Lamu, in his own small plane, he had a fuel leak and had to put down at Malindi airport. He had taken the opportunity to quickly look over the Land Rover which David had parked there before his hasty departure and had already supplied Bob with all the details before we even arrived in Nairobi. This strange coincidental series of meetings between David and Elkan, then Bill and Bob turned out happily and satisfactorily for all of us.

Late one afternoon I was called to the hotel 'phone. "I'm a Sunday Express reporter" said the young man at the other end. "Can I come and talk to you and your family?" I didn't believe it. Three months previously the Sunday Express had printed a story about our proposed journey, but that had been in our home in Kent when we were still in our secure niche surrounded by friends and familiarity. Now we felt adrift in the world and this sudden contact jerked us back to a reality and ties which we had left so long behind us. We told our story honestly and laughed hysterically and not without admiration at the way it was subsequently written up in the newspaper. That night, still smiling at the copy spread on the bed as we washed for supper, a tap on the door interrupted our conversation. David opened it and stepped outside. "I'm looking for my friend" said a girl's voice. I pricked up my ears. "He was staying in this room." "Well he must have moved" suggested David. There was a pause. "If you are looking for a friend, I could stay the night" she replied.

"That's very kind of you, but not tonight, come back tomorrow." He came back in grinning broadly. Outside there were girlish giggles and a hushed conversation, followed by a more determined knock on the door. David signalled at me to open it. I felt a bit mean, the poor girl was speechless when she saw me. "I think you're friend has moved away" I told her. "Perhaps they can help you at the hotel desk." Alone once more I looked at David. "The sooner I get you back to England the better, I reckon. This is not the first time that this has happened." I tried to sound very severe and Victorian, but it didn't come off and we rolled on the bed laughing.

Searching down the list of things to do on the tourist brochure I put a cross by the Masai dancing. Susan rang up and promised to join us and two days later off we went in our own vehicle rather than join the guided tour because it gave us more freedom.

On the road to Lake Naivasha we pinpointed Kikuyu, a small village only a few miles out of our way. We turned off in search of the Scottish Presbyterian Mission where Susan wanted to leave our medicine chest. We had left England substantially equipped to cover most emergencies with intravenous fluids, orthopaedic bandages, antibiotics, sutures and bottles of medicine of all shapes and sizes. Between the six of us we had used three packets of pills for diarrhoea and a small bottle of kaolin and morphine. Many times Susan and I had been tempted to hand out our supplies to the poor Missions we had met along the way, but there had always been the fear that disaster was waiting around the corner and after only a small contribution, we had regretfully snapped shut the case and repacked it. Now we felt we could safely hand over all our supplies. The young American Doctor who took delivery of the case was most appreciative.

The location of the dancing was the Meyer's Farm which we had some difficulty in finding. We accidently passed the road and had to drive back up the long hill. Pausing in the centre of the road with the blinker on before I turned right, as I glanced in the driving mirror I saw a car approaching us rapidly from behind, but assumed he would pass us on the left. I let out the clutch and began a slow right turn. Horrified I saw that he was overtaking on the wrong side. Screaming tyres and flying gravel mixed with a blurred vision of black faces and waving hands, flashing white teeth and a shapeless car triggered the driver's automatic response—both my feet trying to force their way through the floor! My five passengers bumped heads and shoulders and shouted with pain as they lurched forwards and then were flung backwards—but we had missed the crash to end all crashes by inches! I sat momentarily frozen at the wheel watching the car continue its weaving, hair-raising path up the hill, before letting out the clutch once more and pulled across into the dusty track which led to the farm. No one spoke. I clenched my teeth, I simply must not be sick. Glancing in the mirror, I caught David's eye, there was nothing to say. After fifteen minutes driving through scrubby bush land, during which our pounding hearts slowed and finally settled, we found the farm. The dancing was obviously a big tourist attraction but nevertheless worthwhile because of its authenticity, and the farm itself a beauty spot with immaculate lawns and flower beds.

The Masai had their own large reserved area of farm land and we drove on to the training camp of the young warriors, who spent 8 years training and living apart from the nearby village, beginning at the age of 12 years. In the village women with clean-shaven heads and beaded collars and bangles nursed their children and posed for the numerous clicking cameras among their mud huts and invited us to inspect the interior of one hut with its narrow winding entrance, so built to prevent the young heifers from getting in.

Following the other groups of overseas visitors we perched on rough wooden seats and flat stones as the dancers collected within the compound and started a low chant. These tall lithe young men each wore a short piece of cloth like a skirt and their slim bodies were covered with intricate designs. Their hair was long and apparently their pride and joy but to us did not look like hair at all for it was plastered with burnt red clay and then dressed in a selection of complicated styles. Some had innumerable tiny plaits and others heavy bangs across their foreheads with a high bouffant crown. They often paused to titivate or rearrange a friend's hair that seemed to be slightly out of place during the dancing. One or two had shaved heads a sign or recent death within his family.

The dancing began with their famous high jumping on the spot and we marvelled at their agility and performance on a diet of milk and blood. Moving into two lines they danced forward chanting 'Ahhmm, Ahhmm', continuing the rhythm for half an hour as they demonstrated their various dances, each with a simple forward and backward movement of the head, which seemed almost disconnected from the rest of their spine.

They were followed by another tribe, a much shyer and more modest people, who wore ankle length skirts and had less decoration on their bodies. Both tribes had beautiful, fine features and appealing majesty. There seemed no end to the dancing and the low melodious music but the organisers suddenly asked us to gather up our belongings and depart. They explained that as long as any spectators remained the dancers would continue, for hours if necessary, working themselves up into a state of frenzy and physiological imbalance. The continuous hyperventilation inevitably resulted in sever vomiting and impaired consciousness.

Fingering the few souvenir necklaces we had bought, we drove behind a large lorry carrying lengths of timber back to Nairobi. As we watched, some fine-looking pieces of wood worked loose and were obviously within minutes of falling off. We widened the gap and watched. As the first piece clattered onto the road, we pulled in. David leapt out, picked it up and we stowed it in the back. Behind us an English group of overlanders in a Volkswagen caravette slowly overtook us having observed our activities and gave us a wave and a thumbs up. As the next plank duly fell off the lorry, they stopped and claimed it. It became a great game and very hilarious as we alternated with them for booty. Old habits die hard! It was some time before it dawned on us that we no longer needed a wood patrol and really had no use for our fine collection now that our gypsy life was over—but we found willing hands to accept it when we returned to the Hotel.

Our travels were over. We packed our grubby bags and strange collection of luggage, sixteen pieces in all, into the Land Rover and drove out to Bob and Heather's for supper.

Bob had kindly offered to run us to the airport before taking over ownership of the Land Rover. So here we were, brown and healthy and well rested. Strangely enough we were not longing to get home. We had missed our friends very much but after three months we had broken loose from the everyday mundane routine that had threatened to strangle the joy out of each day. David and I were certainly not looking forward to snapping on the chains and sinking back into the 'work, eat, sleep and worry' routine that tends to sweep like the foaming tide over so many lives. "Go and get it out of your systems" people had told us. "Squash the wander bug once and for all. Satiate this restless emotion that leaves each day feeling unfulfilled."

We had gone a long way to achieve this. We had seen a lot, learnt a great deal and met many delightful people. But our appetite had increased, not shrunk. Nevertheless, as a family we had experienced a great togetherness and as a couple David and I returned even more deeply in love.

About the Author

DOCTOR MAUREEN MC Mullan was born (Maureen Johnson) in August 1936. She was educated in York and showed considerable acting ability, becoming involved in the local repertory company. She also however excelled in her school work and the teachers involved persuaded her to take on the challenge of training for a degree in medicine.

Maureen was accepted for training at the University of Edinburgh Medical School in 1955 and qualified in 1961. During her years in Edinburgh she met David Mc Mullan, an R.A.F. Pilot Officer stationed locally. They married in late 1961 in York and Maureen moved to Kent, David's home county, to take up a post as surgeon in Westhill, Dartford, then for many years as a General Practitioner in West Kent. She lived in Tatsfield on the Kent Surrey border and had three children; Peter, Sean and Sarah Jane.

As well as running a busy home with three children and following her career in medicine Maureen spent many happy hours with her husband David, sailing their catamaran Snowgoose of Kent in the English Channel and as far as the Baltic and Bay of Biscay. Her adventurous spirit was responsible for the unusual family expedition across the Sahara and central Africa in 1974.

Maureen in her later years suffered from an almost incurable addiction and finally took her own life in January 1990, three years after she and David had retired to Javea in Spain.

Lightning Source UK Ltd.
Milton Keynes UK
UKOW040427010513

210019UK00003B/171/P